Ultimate
SOAP
CARVING

Easy, Oddly Satisfying Techniques
for Creating Beautiful Designs

MAKIKO SONE

QUARRY

Brimming with creative inspiration, how-to projects, and useful information to enrich your everyday life, Quarto Knows is a favorite destination for those pursuing their interests and passions. Visit our site and dig deeper with our books into your area of interest: Quarto Creates, Quarto Cooks, Quarto Homes, Quarto Lives, Quarto Drives, Quarto Explores, Quarto Gifts, or Quarto Kids.

First Published in 2019 by Quarry Books, an imprint of The Quarto Group,
100 Cummings Center, Suite 265-D, Beverly, MA 01915, USA.
T (978) 282-9590 F (978) 283-2742 QuartoKnows.com

Quarry Books titles are also available at discount for retail, wholesale, promotional, and bulk purchase. For details, contact the Special Sales Manager by email at specialsales@quarto.com or by mail at The Quarto Group, Attn: Special Sales Manager, 100 Cummings Center, Suite 265-D, Beverly, MA 01915, USA.

10 9 8 7 6 5 4 3 2 1

ISBN: 978-1-63159-724-4

Digital edition published in 2019

Library of Congress Cataloging-in-Publication Data available

Templates for use with the projects in this book can be downloaded at www.quartoknows.com/page/ultimate-soap-carving

Design and Page Layout: Mattie Wells
Photography: Makiko Sone

Printed in China

The projects and templates that appear in this book are protected by copyright and may be copied for personal use only. Please use appropriate caution. The author and publisher are not responsible for any injuries associated with using the equipment or following the instructions included in this book.

This book is dedicated to
miracles in my life.

Contents

3: CARVING PROJECTS - - - - - - - - - -54

Introduction

Soap carving is the skill of carving figures such as beautiful flowers, cute animals, or even pretty accessories like sporty high-tops and handbags in soap using a few basic tools. There are some simple guidelines for cutting the soap to create the petals and patterns, but they're easy to follow, allowing you to get started quickly.

Soap carving differs from sculpture because the patterns in the soap aren't carved freely. Instead, you'll use the templates supplied in this book to create your designs. You'll start by carving the soap along the outlines of the template to create the basic shape and then fill in the details to bring the figure to life. Using these templates means that anyone can successfully carve the projects in this book. You'll be amazed at what you can create with only a knife and a bar of soap—and how much fun you'll have doing it!

A BRIEF HISTORY OF SOAP CARVING

Soap carving is based on traditional fruit- and vegetable-carving techniques from Thailand. These techniques were developed in the palaces of Thai kings more than 700 years ago. Using these techniques, court ladies would use a long, pointed knife to carve beautiful flowers and animals in fruits and vegetables, such as watermelons, honeydew melons, papayas, carrots, and pumpkins.

Though fruit and vegetable carving began as an art of the palace, it spread among ordinary Thai people in modern times. According to Nidda Hongwiwat's book, Vegetable and Fruit Carving, in the 1930s a school of home economics was established, with fruit and vegetable carving among the courses taught. Many teachers throughout Thailand enrolled in a year-long training course, which allowed the craft to spread widely.

Because the carved fruits and vegetables don't last long, though, some artists replaced them with bar soap. Though the medium has changed, the traditional techniques are still used.

Carving using both soap and fruit and vegetables as a medium spread to Japan and has become increasingly popular over the last twenty years. Because fruits such as watermelon and papaya aren't affordable in Japan—its climate isn't tropical—soap carving is a popular alternative to carving with tropical fruits.

USING CARVED SOAP

Once you've created your mini-masterpiece, you can use it in a number of ways.

- **Treat yourself!** You can use your carved soap just as you would regular soap. It's the perfect way to pamper yourself on a daily basis. I like using handmade soap, and I started soap carving because I wanted to carve beautiful flowers and delicate patterns in the handmade soap I was already using.

- **Make special gifts for family and friends.** Cute soaps make great, inexpensive gifts for any occasion, including birthdays, graduations, weddings, and other celebrations. Give a hand-carved bar to cheer up a sick friend or welcome a new neighbor to the community. Invited to a dinner party? Instead of a bottle of wine or box of chocolates, surprise your hosts with a beautiful bar of hand-carved soap. Your family and friends will appreciate the unique gift and the fact that you made it yourself.

- **Use the carved soap in an arrangement.** You can make stunning flower arrangements with your carved soap flowers. Arrange the soap flowers like real flowers in a small pot or vase. You can also make an adorable flower wreath with your carved soap flowers (see page 96).

BENEFITS OF SOAP CARVING

If you're wondering if soap carving is for you, consider the following:

- **It's an inexpensive hobby that doesn't require a lot of tools or special materials.** Of course, you'll need soap (you'll find guidance on selecting the best choices for carving in Chapter 1), and you'll also want to invest in a quality carving knife, which will make your hobby much easier and more fun. After that, there are just a few additional tools—some of which you likely already own—that will help you to do the finer carving and sculpting work.

- **It's good for you!** Bar soap is softer than other carving materials such as wood and stone, so it can be cut and carved smoothly and easily. Because of this, many people find soap carving relaxing. It's a great way to unwind after a busy day, and the act of focusing on the soap and the figure you're creating can be meditative and peaceful.

- **You can use your carving skills on other mediums.** Once you learn the technique of soap carving, you can use these same skills to carve beautiful flowers and pretty animals out of fruits and vegetables. Try carving a watermelon or honeydew melon into a fun shape to create a unique centerpiece for your table at your next party!

- **You can sell your creations.** If you find that you really enjoy soap carving, you might want to consider turning your hobby into a small business. Soap flower arrangements, in particular, are often very popular items to sell. A small stand at a farmers' market selling your carved soaps could become a unique and popular stop for customers.

ADVANTAGES OF CARVING SOAP VERSUS MOLDING SOAP

If you want to make cute soap, you could use a mold rather than a carving knife. It's easy to make cute soap with a mold, but there are some distinct advantages to carving soap.

- **If you can do soap carving, you can use those same skills to carve fruits and vegetables, too.** On the other hand, although you can make a rose-shaped soap with a mold, you can't make a carrot rose and a potato rose. This is the most important difference. In addition to the fruits and vegetables, soft candles can be carved in the same way as soap. Soft candles are made for carving.

- **When you carve soap, you can make your desired shape in different sizes according to your preference**, such as a small or large rose or leaf. (Each template in this book comes in two sizes for this reason.) With a soap mold, you're limited to the size of the mold. With soap carving, you can also carve letters in the soap, which allows you to add initials, names, or messages. You can even use your carving skills to customize molded or store-bought soap. Some people make a giant soap bar to carve a large object.

- **You can carve not only store-bought soap, but also handmade soap and molded soap.** However, molded soap is usually made with melt-and-pour soap, which is similar to glycerin soap. It's easy to make cute soap with melt-and-pour soap, but melt-and-pour soap doesn't lather well and it has weaker cleansing power. This is why commercial opaque soap and hand-made soap are more commonly used than melt-and-pour soap.

  Ready to begin? Turn the page for an introduction to the materials and tools you'll need to start making your very own fun and unique carved soaps.

CHAPTER 1

MATERIALS
& Tools

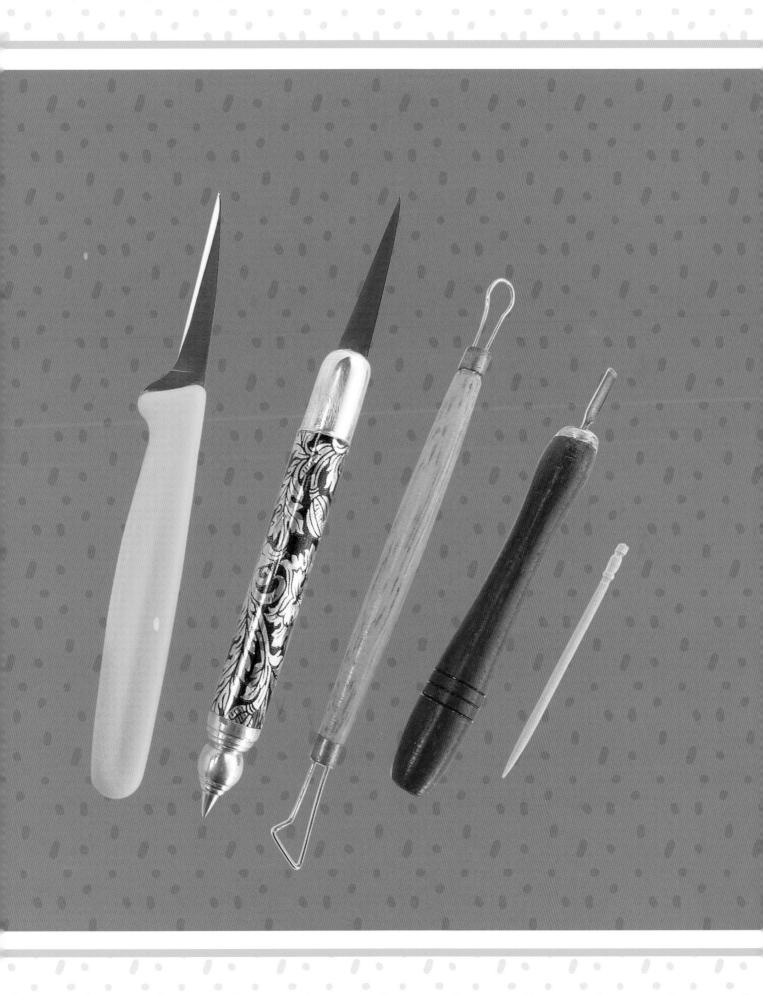

Soap for Carving

You don't need to purchase special soap for carving. You can use commercially made soap that's typically sold in supermarkets, pharmacies, and other retailers. Regardless of the brand or type you use, make sure it's fresh, soft, and moist, because hard, dried-out soap is difficult to carve properly.

Keep these recommendations in mind when choosing soap for carving:

- **Texture.** The soap should be soft, moist, smooth, and fine. Don't use exfoliating soaps.

- **Shape.** Choose soaps that are large and thick so they're easier to carve. I use 3-ounce (85-gram) or 5-ounce (142-gram) bars.

- **Color.** Colored soap is great for carving. Color can enhance a design and emphasize the details in a carved pattern. If your choice of colors is limited, or if you want to customize your designs, you can apply color to carved soap (see page 46 for details).

STORING SOAP

As a general rule, you should purchase soap for carving that's well-packaged; ideally, it should be sealed in plastic. To keep soap from drying out, leave it in its original packaging until you're ready to carve it.

You can wrap loose soaps (including original packaged soaps) in plastic wrap, then store them in a resealable plastic bag or a covered plastic container. To help keep the soaps from drying out, add a tiny bit of water to the bag or container. You can also use this storage method for small pieces of soap that accumulate during carving.

TYPES OF SOAP

In addition to basic commercially made opaque soap that's usually used for carving, there are a few other options to be aware of.

- Once you've gained some carving experience, you might want to try working with **transparent** or **glycerin soap.** Transparent soap is beautiful, but it's hard to carve because it's very sticky, as the glycerin is a humectant, which retains moisture. But, if you make a mistake, transparent soap is easy to melt and harden; though it will be more white than the original soap. Note that **handmade melt-and-pour soap** is very similar to transparent soap in terms of handling.

- Handmade cold-process soap and handmade hot-process soap can be used for carving, but both types are often dry and hard. After they're made, these soaps are usually air dried for long periods in order to evaporate the liquid ingredients so the bars won't soften or melt. If you want to try carving handmade soap, shop for fresh bars, which will likely be softer, or you can soften it before carving (see page 20).

- Typically, soap made locally within your country or region will be fresher than imported soap.

Tools for Carving Soap

CARVING KNIVES

There are two types of carving knives, which are distinguished by the shape of the blade.

- **Bird's beak knife.** This type of knife has a curved spine and a long cutting edge like a bird's beak. The blade of the bird's beak knife is often made of stainless steel. The handle is often constructed of plastic or wood, which makes the bird's beak knife lightweight.

- **Classic carving knife.** This type of knife has a long V-shaped blade and is the kind traditionally used in Thai carving. The cutting edge is usually one side of the blade. The blade of the classic knife is steel or stainless steel. Steel blades are usually very thin and flexible (though very thin stainless steel blades are available, too). The handle of the classic knife is made of aluminum, stainless steel, brass, or wood. An aluminum or wood handle is lightweight. Professional carving artists often use the classic carving knife with a flexible blade.

You can choose either the bird's beak knife or the classic carving knife for the projects in this book. I prefer the bird's beak knife, which is what you'll see throughout the project photos.

Purchasing and Caring for Your Knife

Regardless of whether you choose the bird's beak or the classic knife design, there are many sorts of blades available, and there are differences in the thickness and length of the blade. Generally, cheaper knives tend to have thicker blades, while knives with thin blades are more expensive. You can find a large selection of carving knives online; unfortunately, they are seldom sold at retail stores.

Classic carving knives were originally used for carving fruits or vegetables such as watermelons, honeydew melons, and pumpkins, so I think the blade of the carving knife is too long to carve small soap.

The length of the blade for both the bird's beak knife and the classic carving knife is usually 1¾" to 2" (4.5 cm to 5 cm). A carving knife with a blade of more than 2" (5 cm) is not recommended for soap carving.

Note that you can probably do very simple soap carving with a craft knife (the type used with paper). However, compared to using a carving

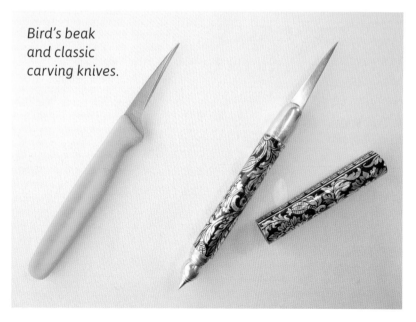

Bird's beak and classic carving knives.

CARVING SOAP WITH KIDS: SAFETY TIPS

Soap carving is a craft that kids will enjoy, and can even use for school projects. Soap is soft, so it's much easier and safer to carve than wood or stone. However, a carving knife is very sharp, so you'll need to follow some guidelines for carving soap with kids.

- **Adult supervision required.** Any time a child uses a sharp object, adult supervision is required. There are recommended carving knife alternatives listed below, but they should only be used in the presence of an adult.

- **Use soft soap.** It's very dangerous for anyone, especially children, to carve hard soap. Carving hard soap could cause the carving knife to easily slip, resulting in an injury. Even when working with soft soap, to avoid injury be mindful not to hold the soap near where you're planning to carve it.

- **Use a carving knife for kids.** As an alternative to a classic carving knife, you can purchase a kid's carving knife, whose blade isn't as sharp. These knives can be found online.

- **Use a craft knife.** Simple soap carving projects can be done with a craft or hobby knife instead of the carving knife. These are easy to find in most craft stores. Note that a utility knife is not recommended because the blade could snap off during carving.

- **Wear safety gloves.** For additional safety, kids should wear a safety glove on the hand they use to hold the soap as they carve (usually their nondominant hand).

- **Store knives securely.** Always keep carving knives out of reach of small children and pets. *Note:* As with all knives, be sure to keep the knives you use for your soap carving—as well as any additional sharp tools—out of the reach of children.

knife, it's very exhausting to carve more complicated projects with a craft knife.

If you're working with a knife that's a bit longer than you'd like, you might try wrapping the base of the blade with a strip of sheet metal, fabric, or tissue paper to protect your fingers. Alternatively, you can shorten a steel blade a bit with a metal file. (A stainless-steel blade will be too hard to shorten.)

How to Sharpen a Dull Carving Knife

You can use 1,000- to 2,000-grit sandpaper to sharpen your carving knife when it becomes dull. First, wet the sandpaper with water and then place it on the edge of a flat work surface. Put the knife blade on the sandpaper and move the knife to the knife spine. Repeat as needed on both sides of the blade. Apply some oil to the knife blade to keep it from rusting if stored for a long time.

ADDITIONAL CARVING TOOLS

In addition to the knife you'll use to do most of your carving, you'll need the following tools:

- **Paring knife.** The paring knife is used to cut the soap roughly (such as when you're cutting out a basic outline) or to slice the soap in half horizontally. You can use a common paring knife.

Paring knives

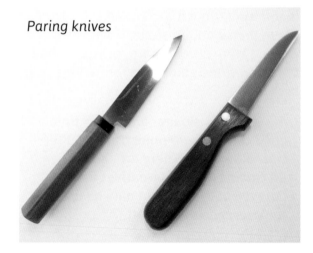

- **Carving gouges.** Carving gouges are used to carve curling petals. You'll be amazed at how easy it is to carve realistic petals with carving gouges. These gouges are sold in sets; the V-tool and U-gouge are often used for soap carving, and there is also a W-tool for carving a wavy petal.

Carving gouges

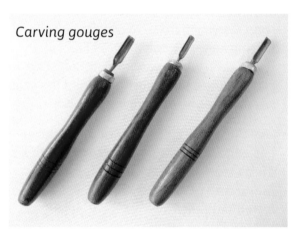

- **Sculpting tool.** A sculpting tool is used to scrape inside the soap or flatten it. It is often used for soap cutwork. You can use a small spoon, such as a teaspoon, a wax carving spatula, or a metal ear pick instead of a sculpting tool.

Sculpting tools

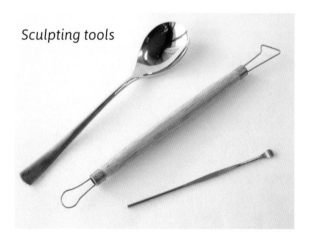

Other Supplies

- **Toothpicks.** Toothpicks are used for drawing outlines on the soap or making small holes in the soap.

- **Cookie cutters.** You can cut out the soap into fancy shapes using cookie cutters. It's easier than cutting with a carving knife. And you can cut a circle for the center bud using a circle cookie cutter on the top of the soap.

- **Pins.** You can use pins to make small holes in the soap. And when you trace the template into the soap, you'll use pins to attach the template.

- **Craft glue, adhesive, or hot glue gun.** If you're planning on displaying your carved soap rather than using it, you can use craft glue or adhesive for adding decorations such as beads. And if a piece of soap accidentally breaks off while you're carving, you can reattach the broken piece with glue to fix it. Any craft glue or adhesive sold for use with paper, fabric, or wood will work.

- **Awl.** You'll need an awl to make small and long holes such as a hole for a stem in a flower bottom.

- **Cutting board.** When you cut the soap with a paring knife, a cutting board will protect your work surface.

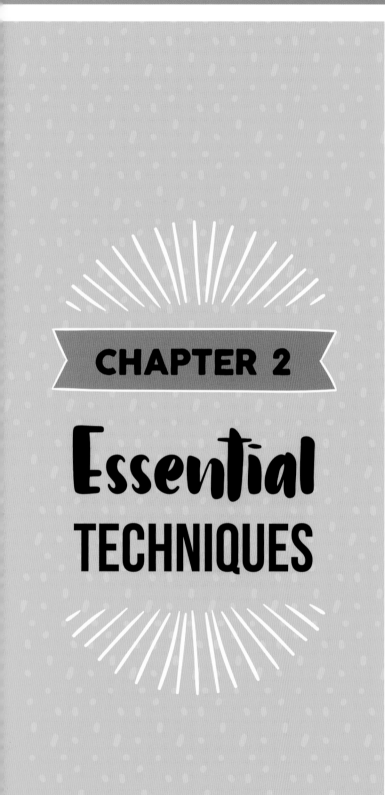
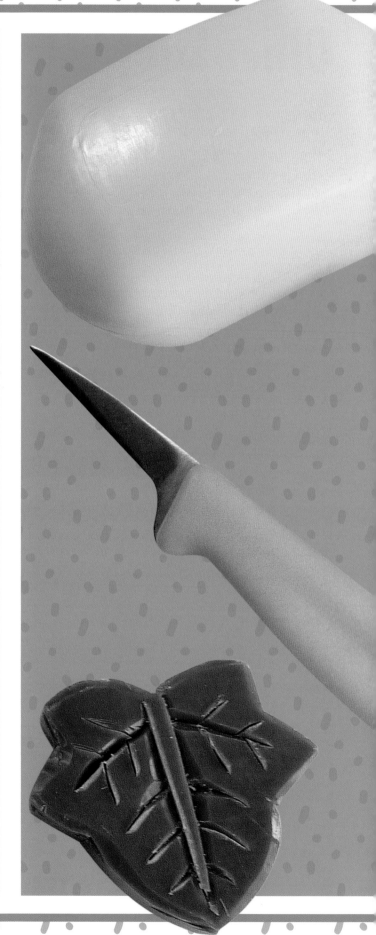

CHAPTER 2

Essential
TECHNIQUES

Getting Started

Once you've chosen your soap and assembled the knives and other supplies you'll be using, there are a few steps you'll need to take before you begin carving the projects in Chapter 3. Spend some time with the following quick primer, which will guide you through preparing and softening your soap for carving, holding your carving knife correctly, and working with the templates in this book. Then try your hand at the projects in the Carving Lessons section, which will help you develop the carving skills you need to create the basic shapes and patterns on which the projects in Chapter 3—as well as all soap-carving designs—are based. Finally, we'll explore some optional techniques to personalize your carvings, such as adding color, decorating with beads and rhinestones, and packaging them creatively to make unique and beautiful gifts.

PREPARING TO CARVE

Before you start carving, you'll need to slice off the top of your soap to create a smooth, flat surface. This is especially important if the brand name of the soap is engraved on the surface. But even if the soap isn't engraved, you'll still want to smooth the surface because, otherwise, it will be a bit dry and crumbly, which isn't ideal for carving. By slicing off the top, you'll be left with a shiny surface.

The one exception to this rule is that you don't need to slice off the top when carving three-dimensional flowers. This type of flower doesn't need a flat surface.

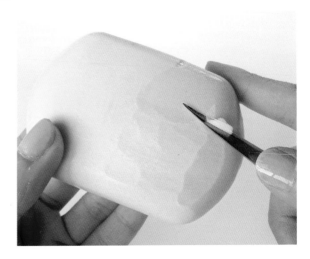

SOFTENING SOAP

Sometimes, despite carefully selecting a soap, you'll discover that it's hard, dry, and crumbly when you try to carve it. Not only does this make carving difficult, but because a knife will easily slip off hard soap, trying to carve it can be dangerous. If your soap is too hard, try these tips for softening it.

- **If your soap is a bit hard:** First, wrap the soap in a wet cloth. Place it in a 500 to 600 watt microwave and warm it for 10 to 15 seconds. If it's still too hard, microwave it for another 10 to 15 seconds. You can repeat this for a total of three cycles per bar of soap. (Be careful not to microwave it for too long or the soap could explode!) Once warmed, carve it quickly.

- **If your soap is extremely hard and dry:** First, wrap the soap in a wet cloth, and then wrap it twice with plastic wrap. Set it aside for at least a week or until softened. I recommend using a cloth made from a chemical fiber, such as rayon or polyester, as moist cotton cloth is likely to develop

» **TIP**

All soap tends to be cool and hard in the winter. An easy solution is to simply warm the soap in your microwave for 10 to 15 seconds. In this case, it's not necessary to wrap the soap in a wet cloth.

mold. If you choose to use a cloth made from cotton, remove the soap within a week. Also, note that handmade soap softens more easily than commercial soap, so it should be soft enough to carve in about five days.

HOLDING A CARVING KNIFE CORRECTLY

It's important to hold your knife correctly as you carve your soap. Depending on the task, you'll want to use one of these two grips.

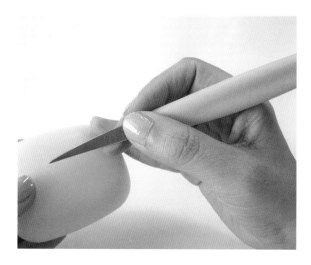

Pen grip. For this grip, hold your carving knife like a pen, using your ring finger for support and to keep the knife from slipping. Use this grip when carving delicate curved lines, patterns, and indents, and when you hold the knife at a right angle.

Handle grip. Grip the handle with your thumb, middle finger, ring finger, and little finger. Use your index finger for support and control and to keep the blade from slipping. Cut or slice the soap away from you, pushing the knife with your thumb. Use the handle grip when you're slicing off or smoothing the surface of the soap.

WORKING WITH THE TEMPLATES

Templates are included at the back of this book for all the projects that require them. For most projects, there are two sizes of each template. The small template is for 3-ounce (85-gram) bars of soap. The large template is for 5-ounce (142-gram) bars. Choose a template based on the size of your soap. Then follow these two simple steps.

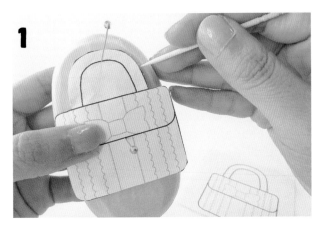

Photocopy and cut out the template and pin it to the soap. Then, using a pointed tool such as a toothpick or an awl, trace around the edge of the template onto the soap.

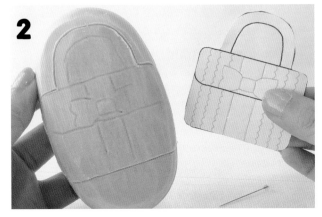

If desired, trace other lines onto the soap, such as a bow, scalloped line, or leaf veins. This step is optional. You don't need to trace all the lines in the template, but you shouldn't leave any traced lines in the finished soap.

SHAPING SOAP FOR CARVING

Once you've traced the outline of your figure onto the soap, you're ready to begin shaping it.

- Lightly cut along the edge of the traced lines with a carving knife. Then roughly cut out the shape with a paring knife.

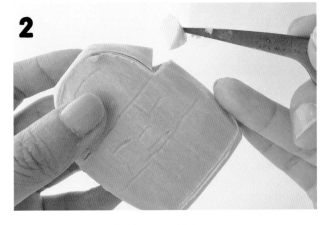

- Using a carving knife, cut off the excess soap around the shape, little by little. Be careful not to trim off too much. Cut off the soap perpendicularly to the top so as to make the bottom and the top into the same shape.

CARVING LESSONS

All soap carving—even the most intricate designs—is based on certain basic shapes and patterns. To prepare yourself for making the projects in Chapter 3, try your hand at the carving lessons on the following pages, which will give you practice in carving popular shapes such as V-shaped grooves, triangular patterns, scalloped edges, waves, petals, and leaves.

V-Shaped Grooves and Incisions

LEAVES

Leaves are a perfect way for beginners to learn soap carving. You will learn the basic techniques of soap carving in this lesson. You can also carve these leaves in relief, which is easier than carving a leaf shape out of soap.

WHAT YOU'LL NEED

» One 3- or 5-ounce (85- or 142-gram) bar soap

» Paring knife

» Carving knife

» Small or Large Leaves template for the Shamrock, Ivy, or Maple Leaf (see page 116)

Traditional Leaf

- To make a traditional leaf (a rose leaf) use a paring knife to roughly cut the soap into a slice of your desired size.
- Use a carving knife to smooth the surface.
- Trim the sliced soap into a leaf shape.

» TIP

There should be no space between each vein. Leaves with wide veins look more beautiful.

- Holding the carving knife at a right angle to the soap, cut two straight lines in the middle of the leaf to create the midrib. Tilting the carving knife, cut the soap along the straight line to remove the soap around the midrib. Do the same on the other side of the midrib.
- Carve wide leaf veins (V-shaped grooves). To do this, first hold the carving knife at a right angle and make a cut on the side of the leaf to create a vein. Next, hold the knife diagonally and make a slant cut along the first cut to remove the soap. Turn your leaf upside down and remove the soap along the first cut in the same way. Do the same to carve the remaining five veins as shown.
- Finally, turn the leaf tip upward and carve small incisions at the edge of the leaf.

Shamrock

- Cut the soap into a slice that's bigger than the shamrock template.
- Photocopy and cut out the template. Trace the shamrock's shape onto the soap.
- Using a carving knife, cut the soap to the shamrock's shape.
- Holding the carving knife at a right angle to the soap, cut four straight lines between the leaves and the stem with the knife point. Cut a straight line in the middle of each leaf, and cut two curved lines in each leaf in a heart shape. Cut off the soap between the right and left leaves to create the stem.

Ivy

- Using the technique described for the shamrock, cut the soap into the ivy shape.
- Carve a midrib in the middle of the leaf using the technique described for the rose leaf.
- Carve eight narrow veins. To do this, hold the knife diagonally and make a slant cut. Turn the ivy upside down and make a slant cut along the previous slant cut to remove the soap. Repeat to carve the other seven narrow veins.
- Using the knife point, cut four curved lines around each of the two veins near the base to create small veins.

Maple Leaf

- Using the technique described for the shamrock, cut the soap into the maple leaf shape.
- Carve a midrib and veins using the technique described for the ivy.

» TIPS

- When cutting off the soap, remove the soap with only two cuts to keep the groove looking neat. If you cut the same spot many times, the unwanted cuts will show and the groove will look messier—and you'll also have more unwanted small soap scraps.

- If you want to cut the same spot, don't cut deeper than the depth of your first cut.

Triangular Patterns

SIMPLE BIRD

Carving a shape, such as a petal, feather, scale, or leaf, between two of the same shapes is the most frequently used way to carve a pattern. Triangular patterns are the easiest shape to carve.

WHAT YOU'LL NEED

» One 3- or 5-ounce (85- or 142-gram) bar soap

» Carving knife

» Small or Large Simple Bird template (see page 116)

» Paring knife

OPTIONAL:
» Two 4 mm plastic eyes

- Thinly slice off the top of the soap, using the template, trace the bird's shape onto the soap. Then cut the soap to the bird's shape.
- Trim the edge around the bird's shape. Place the template on the soap, then trace the shape of the bird's wing with a toothpick. Holding the carving knife at a right angle to the soap, cut the wing lines. Tilting the knife, cut the soap along the lines, and remove the soap to create the wing. Trim the edge around the wing.

- Smooth the soap around the wing, head, and tail. Carve the beak to a pointed shape.
- Cut the first feather: Start to cut from the base of the feather to the tip. Repeat on the other side to create a triangular cut.
- Tilting the carving knife, cut along the triangular shape to remove the soap around the feather.
- To carve this pattern, you should make slightly curved cuts and cut the tip deeply.

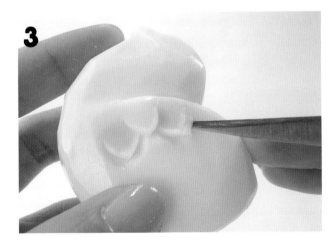

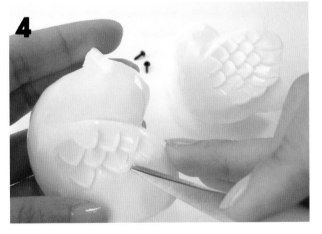

- Carve the second row of feathers: Using the carving knife, smooth the soap where you will carve the feathers of the second row (don't slice off the soap widely), and carve a triangular shape to the lower left side and the lower right side of the first feather.
- When carving the feathers of the second row, make a little gap between the tip of the first feather and the feathers of the second row. This makes the feathers more three-dimensional.

- Carve the third row to the sixth row of feathers in the same way as described in Steps 2 and 3. Then carve the five curved lines at the end of the wing to create long feathers.
- Make a small hole on each side with an awl or toothpick to create the eyes. If desired, attach a plastic eye by gently pushing it into each hole. (Be careful to not to make the eyeholes too big.
- Cut the tip of the triangular shape a bit deeper to easily remove the soap around the triangular shape.
- Cut slightly curved lines for the triangular shapes.

Circular Scalloped Patterns

SCALLOPED BUTTERFLY

This sweet butterfly design, which includes both single- and double-scallop patterns, is a great way to learn these carving configurations.

WHAT YOU'LL NEED

» One 3- or 5-ounce (85- or 142-gram) bar soap

» Carving knife

» Small or Large Butterfly template (see page 117)

» Paring knife

OPTIONAL:

» Six 3 mm pearl beads

» Artificial flower stamens

1

- Thinly slice off the top of the soap. Using the template, trace the butterfly's shape onto the soap.
- Then cut the soap to the butterfly's shape.
- Place the template on the soap, then trace the shape of the butterfly's body with a toothpick.
- Holding the carving knife at a right angle to the soap, cut around the shape of the butterfly's body, then tilt the knife to remove the soap from around the body.

2

- Make short incisions on the top and bottom of the body to separate the right wing and the left wing.
- Smooth the soap around the body to create the scalloped patterns.
- Use the template to mark two equally spaced dots in each forewing and a dot in each hindwing.
- Holding the knife at a nearly right angle, cut half circles between the dots to create the scalloped patterns.
- Then, tilting the knife, remove the soap around the scalloped cuts.

3

Using the technique described in Step 2, carve the double-scallop pattern on the outer area of each wing.

4

- Carve two holes in the double-scallop patterns in each forewing and a small hole and a pointed oval in each hindwing.
- Make small holes along the double-scallop patterns with a pin or a toothpick.
- Carve three pointed ovals in each forewing and two pointed ovals around the body in each hindwing.
- *Optional:* Decorate the wings with beads and add artificial flower stamens to create antennae.

» TIPS

- **Carve the right and left scallop patterns symmetrically.**
- **When you cut the half circles, turn the soap in the opposite direction of the knife.**

Delicate Waves

PURSE

Delicate waves carved in soap look like edges of lace. This simple technique allows you to dress up your soap carvings with gorgeous, fancy details, as in these cute purse carvings.

WHAT YOU'LL NEED

» One 3- or 5-ounce (85- or 142-gram) bar soap

» Carving knife

» Small or Large Purse template (see page 117)

» Paring knife

OPTIONAL:

» One 8 mm pearl bead

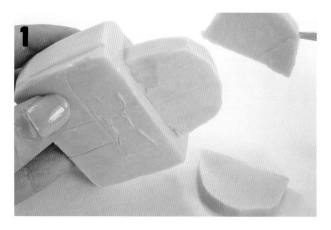

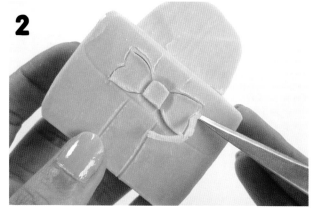

- Using a carving knife, thinly slice off the top of the soap to create a flat surface.
- Photocopy and cut out the template. Trace the purse's shape onto the soap.
- Using a paring knife and a carving knife, cut the soap to the purse's shape.
- Using a carving knife, cut off the upper part of the purse to remove the unwanted soap and create a handle.

- Place the template on the soap and trace the shape of the bow with a toothpick.
- Holding the carving knife at a right angle to the soap, cut around the shape of the bow. Tilting the knife, remove the soap from around the bow.

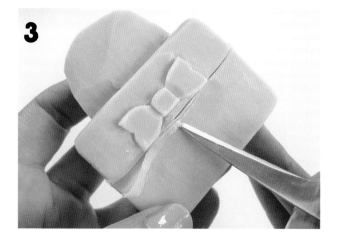

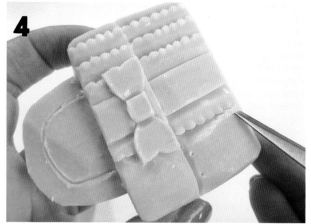

Using the carving knife, smooth the soap around the bow, and then cut the flap under the bow. Tilting the knife, remove the soap around the flap. Smooth the soap under the flap to carve delicate waves.

» TIP

Carve the delicate waves in any size you like, but cut them all the same size.

- Carve two straight lines to create a wide ribbon in the middle of the purse.
- Carve delicate waves. To do this, use a toothpick to lightly mark dots in the places where you will carve the delicate lines. Holding the knife at a nearly right angle, repeatedly move the knife point up and down a little bit from the marked dots, cutting a wavy line. Then, tilting the knife, cut along the wavy line to remove the soap. Repeat this to carve the other delicate wavy lines.
- Trim around the edge of the purse. Cut out the inside of the handle.
- *Optional:* Carve a small indent in the middle of the bow. Carefully push a pearl bead in it.

Complex Floral Designs

DAHLIA

Let's try carving a flower with a center bud. If you can carve a center bud, you will be able to carve various flowers such as a dahlia, rose, zinnia, calendula, chrysanthemum, etc. The dahlia is carved using the center bud and the triangular petals.

WHAT YOU'LL NEED

» One 3- or 5-ounce (85- or 142-gram) bar soap
» Paring knife
» Carving knife
» Toothpick

- Using a paring knife, roughly cut the soap into a dome shape that's 2" (5 cm) in diameter and 1" (2.5 cm) in height.
- Smooth the surface of the soap with a carving knife.

- Using a toothpick, draw a ¾" (1.8 cm) circle in the center of the dome.
- Holding the carving knife at a right angle, cut the circle about ½" (1.2 cm) deep to create a center bud.
- Then, slightly tilting the knife, cut around the circle to remove the soap. You can remove the soap on the outside of the circle or on the inside of the circle; either will work.
- Trim the cylinder-shaped center to a small dome shape.

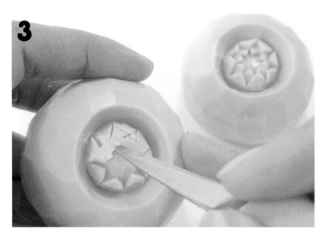

- *Carve the first row of the center bud:* Using a toothpick, lightly divide the center into eight equal parts by marking each part with a short line or dot.
- Cut a pointed petal in each part by making slightly curved cuts. Then, holding the knife nearly horizontally, cut off the soap between the petals.
- *Carve the second row of the center bud:* Cut eight pointed petals. Each petal should be carved between the tips of two petals in the first row. Next, cut off the soap between the petals. Neaten the center.

- *Carve the first layer of the outer petals:* Using a toothpick, lightly divide the area around the center bud into eight equal parts by marking each part with a short line or dot.
- Carve a shallow indent in each part (like a U-shaped trench), and then cut a pointed petal within each indent.
- Remove the soap between the petals. To do this, horizontally cut between the petals, inserting the knife point to the base of the petal. Do the same to remove the soap between the rest of the petals.

5

- *Carve the second layer of the outer petals:* Carve eight shallow indents (or U-shaped trenches) between the petals of the first layer. When you carve these indents, be careful not to cut the petals of the previous layer.
- Then cut eight pointed petals between the petals of the first layer. Cut the petal tip a bit deeper to easily remove the soap between the petals of the next row. Remove the soap between the petals in the same way as described in Step 4.

6

- Carve the third to fifth layer of the outer petals in the same way as described in Steps 4 and 5. Each layer of petals is bigger than the petals of the previous layer. For example, the petals in the third layer are bigger than the petals in the second layer, and the petals in the fourth layer are bigger than those in the third layer.
- Finally, cut off the unwanted soap on the bottom.

» TIP

Carve the petals in the same layer all the same size, but make the petals bigger than the petals of the previous layer.

Complex Floral Designs

ROSE RELIEF

The rose is the most frequently carved flower. There are many variations of the rose, and I've included a few of them in this book. I recommend carving the rose in relief because you'll end up with fewer soap scraps after carving.

WHAT YOU'LL NEED

» One 3- or 5-ounce (85- or 142-gram) bar soap
» Carving knife
» Toothpick

Rose relief in pink transparent soap. This bar of transparent soap is made of melt-and-pour soap.

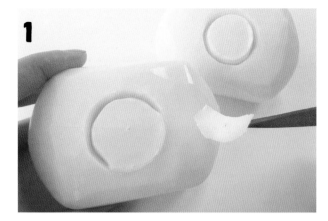

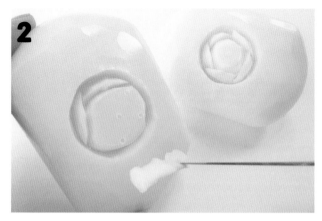

- Using a carving knife, thinly slice off the top of the soap to create a flat surface.
- Draw a circle in the center of the soap with a toothpick (the diameter of the circle should be half of the width of the soap).
- Holding the carving knife at a right angle, cut the circle about ½" (1.2 cm) deep to create a center bud. Then, slightly tilting the knife, cut around the circle to remove the soap. You can remove the soap on the outside of the circle or on the inside of it; either will work.

- *Carve the first row of the center bud:* Begin by trimming around the upper side of the cylinder a bit (don't trim the cylinder to a dome shape). Using a toothpick, mark five dots to divide the top of the center into five equal parts.
- Carve the first petal of the first row. To do this, hold the knife at a nearly right angle to the center and start to cut a little pointed petal from the base of the petal. The petal should be a little bigger than the length divided into five parts. Then make a thin slice to cut off the soap inside of the petal.
- Smooth the soap where you will start to cut the second petal. Carve the second petal so that it slightly overlaps the first petal. Carve the third and fourth petals in the same way as the second petal. Carve the fifth petal so that it overlaps both the first petal and the fourth petal.

- *Carve the second row of the center bud:* Trim the center (inside the first row) to a dome shape. Each petal of the second row is placed between the petals of the previous row. Tilting the carving knife, cut the first petal of the second row, placing it between the first petal and the fifth petal of the previous row. Remove the soap inside the petal, and smooth the soap where you will start to cut the second petal. Carve the second to fifth petals. Each petal slightly overlaps its neighboring petal.
- *Carve the third row of the center bud:* Trim the center (inside the second row) to a lower and smaller dome shape. Carve five petals in the third row as described for the second row.
- *Optional:* You can carve more rows with a fewer number of petals inside the third row.

4

- *Carve the first row of the outer petals:* Carve a shallow indent between the first petal and the fifth petal of the center bud, but be careful not to cut the petals of the center bud. Start to cut from the bottom left of the petal to the tip, then cut from the bottom right of the petal to the tip to create a pointed rose petal. Finally, cut off the soap outside the petal.
- Smooth the soap where you will start to carve the second petal, and carve a shallow indent between the petals of the center bud. Carve a little pointed petal in the same way that you carved the first petal.
- Each petal should be a little bigger than one-fifth of the circumference of the center bud, and slightly overlaping its neighboring petal.

5

6

Carve the second row of the outer petals: Carve a shallow indent between the first petal and the fifth petal of the previous row, but be careful not to cut the petals of the previous row. This row of petals will be a little bigger than the petals of the previous row. Carve the first petal of the second row in the same way as described for the previous row. Then carve the second petal to the fifth petal, placing each petal between the petals of the previous row.

- Smooth the soap around the rose to carve the leaves.
- *Carve ten leaves:* Cut a leaf shape in the upper right corner, and then remove the soap around the leaf. Carve a wide V-shaped indent in the leaf. Then, using the knife point, cut several veins. Smooth around the leaf, and then carve a leaf to both sides of the first leaf in the same way. The first leaf should overlap the two leaves alongside it. Repeat to carve three leaves in the lower left corner. Next, carve two leaves in the lower right corner and two leaves in the upper left corner.
- Finally, smooth out the blanks or uncarved areas. Make sure the height of the blanks is equal.

» TIP

When you carve the indents, be careful not to cut the petals of the previous row. If it is done, the unwanted cut will show.

ESSENTIAL TECHNIQUES

Complex Floral Designs

ROSE STARTING WITH THE OUTER PETALS

There are two ways to carve a three-dimensional rose out of soap: starting with the outer petals or starting at the center. Starting with the outer petals is a little easier. It's also suitable for carving a half-open rose.

WHAT YOU'LL NEED

» One 3- or 5-ounce (85- or 142-gram) bar soap

» Paring knife

» Carving knife

» Toothpick

Using a paring knife, roughly cut the soap into a dome shape that's 2" (5 cm) in diameter and 1" (2.5 cm) in height. Smooth the surface of the soap with a carving knife. The flat side will become the top of the rose and the dome will become the base.

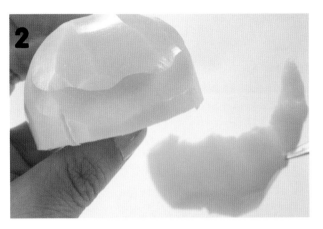

Carve the first row: Using a toothpick, divide the bottom edge of the dome into five equal parts by making short lines or dots to designate each part. Holding the soap with the dome side facing up and tilting the carving knife toward the soap, cut the first petal of the first row. The petal should be wavy and a little bigger than the part divided. Then cut off the soap inside the petal.

Smooth the soap where you will start to carve the second petal. Cut the second petal so that it slightly overlaps the first petal, and then remove the soap inside the petal. Smooth the soap where you will start to carve the third petal, then carve the third petal in the same way as the second petal. Next, carve the fourth and the fifth petals. The fifth petal should overlap both the first and fourth petals.

Carve the second row: Holding the soap with the flat side facing up, smooth around the edge of the center, and then carve the first petal of the second row, placing it between the first petal and the fifth petal of the first row. Next, carve the second to fifth petals in the same way as the first row.

5

Carve the third row: Smooth around the edge of the center (but don't make the center into a dome shape), and then carve the five petals of the third row. Each petal should be placed between the petals of the previous row

6

- *Carve the fourth and fifth rows:* Trim the center (inside the third row) to a small dome shape, and then carve the five petals of the fourth row.
- Next, trim the center to a lower and smaller dome shape, and carve five (or fewer, depending on space) petals in the fifth row.
- *Optional:* You can carve more rows inside the fifth row, if you'd like.
- Finally, slice off the outsides of the petals of the first row to look like rose petals.

» TIPS

- Carve the petals in the same row all the same size, but make the petals smaller than the petals of the outer rows.
- When you cut off the soap inside the petal, don't cut the same spot many times. If you cut inside the petal repeatedly, unwanted cuts will show.

These roses and leaves are carved out of transparent soap. I added stems to the roses and leaves and put them in an egg cup.

Complex Floral Designs

ROSE STARTING AT THE CENTER

This rose looks like a fully open rose. It has only two outer layers, so you can carve it easily and quickly with this method.

WHAT YOU'LL NEED

» One 3- or 5-ounce (85- or 142-gram) bar soap
» Paring knife
» Carving knife
» Toothpick

- Using a paring knife, roughly cut the soap into a dome shape that's 2" (5 cm) in diameter and 1" (2.5 cm) in height. Smooth the surface of the soap with a carving knife.
- Using a toothpick, draw a circle in the center of the soap. The circle's diameter should be about 1¼" (about 3 cm).
- Holding the carving knife at a right angle to the soap, cut the circle about ½" (1.2 cm) deep to create a center bud. Then, slightly tilting the knife, cut around the circle to remove the soap. You can remove the soap on the outside of the circle or on the inside of it; either will work.

- *Carve the first row of the center bud:* Trim around the upper side of the cylinder a bit (don't trim the cylinder into a dome shape). Using a toothpick, divide the top of the center into five equal parts by designating each part with short lines or dots.
- *Carve the five petals of the first row:* To do this, holding the knife at a nearly right angle to the center, cut a wavy petal (like slicing into one side of the cylinder) and remove the soap inside the petal. This is the first petal. Next, carve the second to the fifth petal using the technique described for the first petal. This is similar to the technique described for the center bud of the rose relief (see page 37). The five petals should slightly overlap each other where each petal is slightly bigger than one-fifth the circumference of the cylinder.

» TIPS

- When you carve the indents, be careful not to cut the petals of the previous row. If you cut deeper than the base of the petal, unwanted cuts will show.

- The outer petals of the first layer open at a nearly horizontal angle, while the outer petals of the second layer open downward.

- *Carve the second and third rows of the center bud:* Trim the center (inside the first row) to a dome shape. Then carve five wavy petals in the second row, placing each petal between the petals of the previous row.
- Trim the center (inside the second row) to a lower and smaller dome shape, and then carve five wavy petals in the third row, placing each petal between the petals of the previous row.
- *Optional:* If you'd prefer, you can carve more rows with a fewer number of petals inside the third row.

- *Carve the first layer of the outer petals:* Slightly cut off and lower the height of the soap around the center bud. Carve a shallow wavy indent between the first petal and the fifth petal of the center bud. Tilting the knife, cut a wavy petal in the wavy indent. The petal should be a little bigger than one-fifth of the circumference of the center bud. Then cut off the soap outside the petal.
- Smooth the soap where you will start to carve the second petal, and carve a shallow wavy indent between the petals of the center bud. Carve a second wavy petal that slightly overlaps the first petal.
- Carve the third to fifth petals in the same way.

Carve the second layer of the outer petals: Slightly cut off and lower the height of the soap around the first layer of outer petals. Carve a wavy indent between the first petal and the fifth petal of the previous layer. Lower the edge of the indent so that the carved petal will open downward. Then carve the five wavy petals of the second layer in the same way as you did for the previous layer. The petals of the second layer will be a little bigger than the petals of the previous layer.

Finally, cut off the unwanted soap from the bottom of the rose.

Adding Color

There are several options for coloring carved soap. If you plan to actually use the soap for bathing, you'll need to use skin-safe products for color, such as soap-making colorants, food coloring, or cosmetics. These techniques are shown below.

If your carved soap will only be displayed, you can use any type of coloring, including watercolors, acrylic paints, fabric dyes, or glitter. Once the color is dry, you can seal it with a protective coat of varnish.

USING COSMETICS

WHAT YOU'LL NEED

» **Water or rubbing alcohol**

» **Carved soap**

» **Paintbrush**

» **Makeup sponge**

» **Powdered eyeshadow**

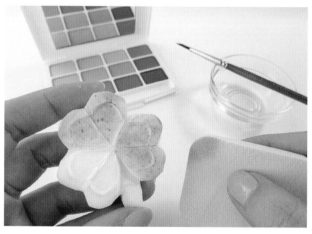

Apply water or rubbing alcohol to an area of the carved soap with the paintbrush. (Alcohol evaporates more quickly than water, so you'll need to work more quickly if you use it.) Use the makeup sponge to apply the eye shadow to the moistened area. Let dry, then repeat as desired.

USING SKIN-SAFE LIQUID COLORANTS

WHAT YOU'LL NEED

» **Skin-safe colorants (soap-making colorants or food coloring)**

» **Water**

» **Paint palette**

» **Carved soap**

» **Paintbrush**

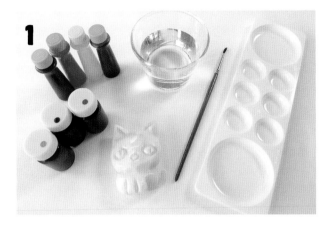

Gather your materials. Both food coloring and soap-making colorants are shown, but only one type of colorant is needed.

Add a very small amount of the colorant to the water and mix thoroughly to create a very light tint. Test the color with a separate piece of soap and then apply it to the carved soap using a paintbrush. To create a darker tint of the same color, gradually add small amounts of colorant to the water. I used the lighter tint to color the cat's body, and the darker tint to enhance the stripes and other details.

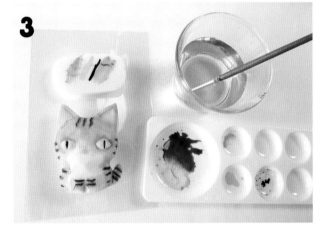

When the soap has absorbed the colored water and the surface is dry to the touch, repeat Step 2 as needed to apply other colors, using clean water to mix each one.

Decorating with Beads

You can beautifully decorate your carved soap with beads, rhinestones, glitter, or stickers. Decorating with these items not only makes the soap more beautiful, but it is also so fun and creative!

If your carved soap will only be displayed, you can use craft glue or craft bond to attach your small decorations. You can attach beads or rhinestones to the soap with fabric or paper glue. Small soap parts (such as a piece that might have accidentally broken off) can be attached to the soap with craft glue, as well.

If you intend to actually use the carved soap and would like to attach beads, carve small holes in your soap and press the beads into them. To add rhinestones, apply a bit of water to the soap using a paintbrush, and then affix the rhinestones to the soap. Glitter also can be added with water using the same technique. If you need to attach a small piece of soap, you can use water, cream soap, or face wash. (Be aware that rhinestones and soap parts attached with water have a greater tendency to fall off.)

MAKING ROOM DECORATIONS

You can also make room decorations such as a flower arrangement, a flower wreath, or a decorative frame with your carved soap. They make perfect gifts. Use craft glue, adhesive, or a glue gun to affix the soap.

For some examples, see pages 78, 89, and 98.

Recycling Soap Scraps

If you have a lot of soap scraps left over from your carvings, try making these easy soaps.

Note that it's very difficult to melt commercial opaque soap and it's also difficult to pour it in a mold. Generally, molded soap is made with melt-and-pour soap. Melt-and-pour soap can easily be melted into liquid in a microwave, but unfortunately the same isn't true for opaque soap. While glycerin soap is similar to melt-and-pour soap, commercial glycerin soap cannot easily be melted into a liquid.

CREAM SOAP

Making cream soap with small flakes of leftover soap is very easy. You can use this cream soap for reattaching soap parts that have broken off and for making soap confectioneries, decorative soaps that need a cream-like facsimile, such as a cream puff or a parfait. Cream soap is also useful for cleaning. (Note that the cream soap won't be smooth enough to pipe like whipped cream.)

WHAT YOU'LL NEED

» **3 ounces (85 grams) soap flakes**

» **¾ cup (175 ml) water**

» **Jar or container with a lid**

» **Spoon**

» TIP

It's very difficult to make liquid soap from pieces of bar soap. If you dilute this cream soap with water, it will turn to gel after a while. The ingredients of liquid soap are different from those of bar soap, and liquid soap is originally a watery substance.

Put the soap flakes in the jar and add the water (pictured on the left). Close the lid of the jar and leave it for 2 to 3 days at room temperature. Then mix it well with a spoon (pictured on the right). If you use your cream soap to make soap confectioneries, let it dry and set for 2 to 3 days.

REBATCHED BAR SOAP

You can make a rebatched, or new, bar of soap with your cuttings, then use it for carving. Since they would be too difficult to grate, soap flakes or tiny pieces of soap aren't recommended for creating rebatched bar soap.

Glycerin makes the soap moist and tough. Sugar helps to increase bubbles and lather.

(Left) A freshly made rebatched soap bar; (center) rebatched bar soap smoothed with a carving knife; (right) a rebatched bar soap carving.

WHAT YOU'LL NEED

» **2.8 to 3.2 ounces (80 to 90 grams) soap pieces (from a block or bar)**

» **2 teaspoons (9 grams) sugar**

» **2 teaspoons (10 ml) glycerin or 3 teaspoons (15 grams) transparent soap**

» **2 tablespoons (30 ml) water**

» **Grater**

» **Stainless steel or heat-resistant glass mixing bowl**

» **Spoon or spatula**

» **Ramekin (about 3¾" [9.5 cm] in diameter) or other heat-resistant container**

» **Plastic wrap**

1

- Finely grate the pieces of soap into powder. In the mixing bowl, combine the soap powder and sugar. Line the ramekin with plastic wrap, allowing the plastic wrap to overhang the top.
- Place the bowl of soap in or over a pot of hot water to warm it. Alternately, you can use an induction cooker on low heat, about 170°F (75°C).

2

- Pour the glycerin or transparent soap and the water into the mixing bowl. Stir for several minutes or until the mixture turns into a paste. Quickly transfer the paste to the ramekin and fill it as tightly as possible.
- Cool at room temperature or in the refrigerator for 1 to 2 hours.
- Once cooled, hold the plastic wrap and remove the soap from the ramekin. Remove the plastic wrap from the soap. Allow the soap to dry at room temperature for 1 to 2 days.
- If you won't be carving the rebatched soap right after it dries, store it wrapped in plastic wrap.
- *Optional:* Smooth the surface of the rebatched soap with a carving knife.

SOAP BALL

It's very easy to make a soap ball! The texture of the soap ball is too rough to carve, so use it for bathing.

WHAT YOU'LL NEED

- » **3 ounces (85 grams) soap flakes (your desired color)**
- » **4 teaspoons (20 ml) water**
- » **Small container**
- » **Plastic wrap**
- » **Spoon or spatula**
- » **Towel**

(Left) A freshly made soap ball; (right) a soap ball smoothed by a carving knife.

- Line the container with plastic wrap. Add the soap flakes and water to the container and stir to combine. Using the plastic wrap, shape the mixture into a ball. Warm it in a 500-watt microwave for 20 seconds.
- Using a towel to protect your hands, quickly squeeze the soap ball firmly with both bands to compress its shape and fill any gaps. (Be careful, it's very hot.)
- Set it aside to cool at room temperature or in the refrigerator. When cool, remove the plastic wrap and let the soap ball dry at room temperature for 1 to 2 days.

Gift-Giving Ideas

Cute carved soaps make amazing gifts that will actually be used! Here are three quick ideas for wrapping and presenting your carved soap. They are suitable for any occasion. You don't necessarily need to use transparent plastic bags or boxes, but doing so allows the recipient of the gift to display it conveniently and cleanly.

USING A FLAT BAG

This gift-wrap option is quick and easy.

WHAT YOU'LL NEED

» Carved soap
» Paper filler, piece of paper or paper doily, and/or a cupcake liner

» Flat bag
» Embellishments, such as ribbons and bows

Basic. I recommend this presentation for simple shaped soaps. Line the inside of the flat bag with a piece of paper or a paper doily and place the soap on top. Close the bag and decorate with embellishments as desired.

With a Paper Cupcake Liner. This easy presentation can be used for more complex-shaped soap such as flowers. Put a small amount of shredded paper filler in a cupcake liner, and then line it with the paper doily. Place the cupcake liner in the bag and nestle the carved soap inside the doily. Close the bag and decorate with embellishments as desired.

USING A GIFT BOX

Another great way to present your carved soap is to wrap it in a gift box. Get creative and try different types of boxes, such as transparent or paper boxes in various shapes. I recommend using a box for soaps carved with delicate designs, because the box will provide some additional protection for this fragile soap. Some delicately carved soap presented in a gorgeous box makes an excellent gift for your friends and family.

WHAT YOU'LL NEED

» Paper doily, deco mesh, or tissue paper

» Gift box

» Double-sided tape

» Carved soap

» Embellishments, such as ribbons and bows

- If using a paper doily, attach it to the bottom of the gift box with double-sided tape. Then use the tape to attach the carved soap to the doily.
- If using deco mesh or tissue paper, arrange it in the gift box, and then nestle the carved soap on top.
- Close the box and decorate with embellishments as desired.

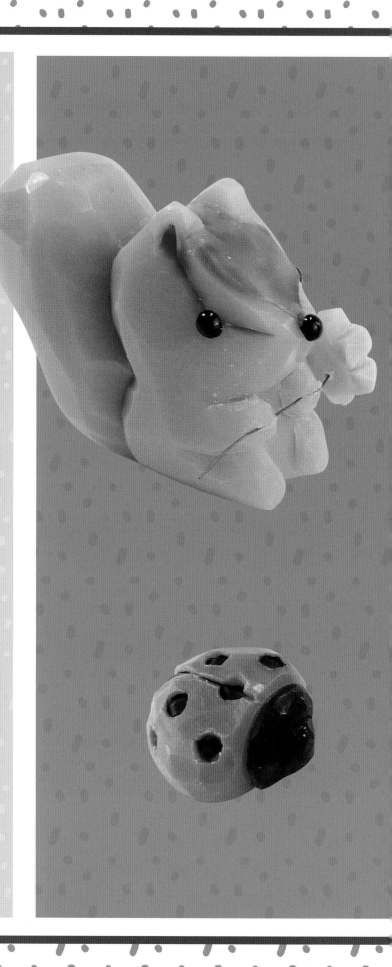

CHAPTER 3

Carving
PROJECTS

Miniature Cactus

The spines of this little cactus are carved with a V-tool, which makes creating them easy and quick. This is a great technique for beginners.

» SKILL LEVEL: EASY

WHAT YOU'LL NEED

» One 3- or 5-ounce (85- or 142-gram) bar soap

» Paring knife

» Carving knife

» Toothpick

» V-tool

» Miniature pot (about 1½" [4 cm] in diameter)

OPTIONAL:

» Small piece of soap in a different color

» Artificial flower stamens

- Using the paring knife, cut the soap into long pieces. The size and the number of soap pieces depend on the size of your pot.
- Using the carving knife, trim the top and sides of the soap pieces to round all the edges and form the stem of the cactus.

- Using a toothpick, divide the top and the side of the soap piece into eight equal parts to create eight V-shaped grooves around the cactus stem.
- To carve a V-shaped groove in each part, make a straight cut in the middle of the outlines and then make two slanting cuts to both sides of the straight cut to remove the soap. Make V-shaped grooves in the other seven parts in the same way. Do the same for the other soap piece(s).

Using a V-tool, carve some cactus spines around the soap piece. To do this, slightly push the V-tool upward in between the grooves to carve each spine. Do the same for the other soap piece(s).

- Place the cacti in the pot. Then cut the soap scraps into tiny pieces and use them to fill in the gaps in the pot.
- *Optional:* Make a cactus flower: Cut out a small flower shape with six petals out of the different colored soap. Next, carve a small inverted cone shape in the center and then carve a shallow indent in each petal. Add a few artificial stamens in the center of the flower. Slightly cut off the bottom of the flower and attach it to the top of the cactus with water or glue.

Lily of the Valley

This lily of the valley can be made with very small soap pieces. Instead of discarding the scraps from a white bar of soap after carving a different project, use them to make this adorable flower.

» **SKILL LEVEL: EASY**

WHAT YOU'LL NEED

» Small pieces of soap (I recommend using white and green)

» Paring knife

» Carving knife

» Craft wire (#26 gauge/0.4 mm)

OPTIONAL:

» Cork coaster, awl, craft wire, adhesive or craft glue, strip of lace ribbon, strip of narrow ribbon

1

- Using the paring knife, cut a piece of white soap into a ¾" (1.8 cm) cube.
- With the carving knife, trim the edge of the cube to create a rounded flower bottom. Then divide the top of the soap into six equal parts and cut small notches around the edge of the soap to form six petals. Repeat for each piece of soap if you're making multiple lilies.

2

- Holding the carving knife at a right angle, carve a small inverted cone shape in the center.
- Tilting the carving knife, carve a shallow indent in each petal. Repeat for each piece of soap.

3

- Trim around the side of each flower to make flared petals.
- Then cut some pieces of the wire to your desired length and slightly fold one end on each piece. The fold will help ensure that the lilies don't come off.
- Make a small hole in the bottom of a flower and insert the folded end of the wire into the hole. (You can use glue to secure the wire.) Repeat for the other flowers. Then twist them together, making a gap between the flowers.

4

- To make a few leaves, cut the green soap into 6 mm slices and trim them into leaves. Carve some straight lines in each leaf.
- *Optional:* Make a hanging décor: Pierce two holes opposite each other (as wide as the lily stem) in a cork coaster and place the stem between the holes. Thread a small piece of wire through each hole and cinch the wire on the reverse side of the coaster to secure the stem. Repeat these steps.
- Glue a strip of lace ribbon around the edge of the coaster. Attach the leaves with glue and make a hole, then thread the narrow ribbon through the hole and tie a knot.

Dachshund

This supercute design is perfect for dog lovers. Make a whole litter of wiener dogs, then customize them with color!

» SKILL LEVEL: EASY

WHAT YOU'LL NEED

» One 3- or 5-ounce (85- or 142-gram) bar soap

» Carving knife

» Small or Large Dachshund template (see page 117)

» Paring knife

» Three 4 mm to 6 mm plastic eyes

1

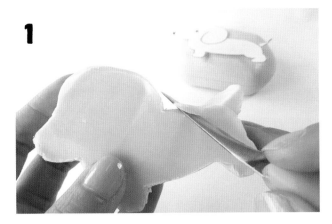

- Use the carving knife to thinly slice away the top of the soap to create a flat surface.
- Photocopy and cut out the template. Trace the dog shape onto your soap.
- Using a paring knife and a carving knife, cut the dog shape out of the soap.
- Trim and shape the edges as needed.

2

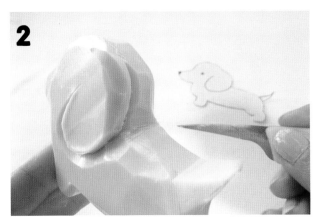

- Place the template on the soap, then trace the dog's ear with a toothpick. Repeat on the other side.
- Cut out the ear shape and remove the surrounding soap, first on one side, then on the other.

3

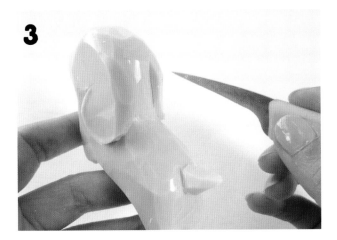

- Remove the soap from between the ears, and then trim the edges of the ears.
- Shape the front and the edges of the face to create a pointed muzzle.
- Trim the tail into a pointed shape.

4

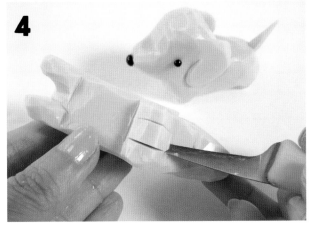

- Carve the legs. Remove the soap from between the legs and trim their edges.
- Make two small eyeholes and a small hole in the end of the nose. Place the plastic eyes in the holes.

Cat

This is the perfect project to experiment with using color. Make the cat with white soap and color it as you like (such as a tabby, calico, bicolor, or ginger cat). Of course, a white cat is pretty, too.

» SKILL LEVEL: EASY

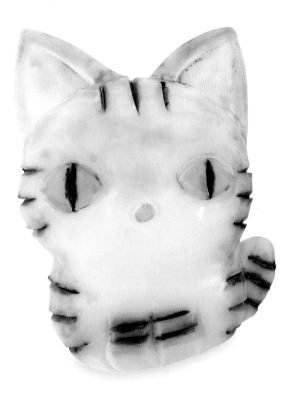
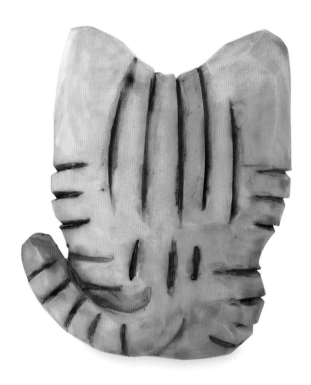

WHAT YOU'LL NEED

» One 3- or 5-ounce (85- or 142-gram) bar soap

» Carving knife

» Small or Large Cat template (see page 118)

» Paring knife

» Colorants

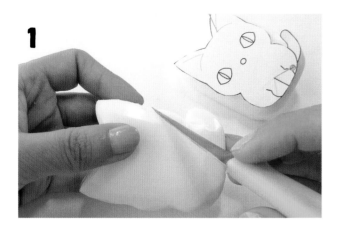

- Use the carving knife to thinly slice away the top and bottom of the soap to create a flat surface.
- Photocopy and cut out the template. Trace the cat shape onto your soap.
- Using a paring knife and a carving knife, cut the cat shape out of the soap.
- Trim and shape the edges as needed.

- Using the carving knife, cut out a thin slice of soap from the front of the ear to create the cat's head. Do the same for the other ear.
- Trim the edge of the head.
- Finally, remove the unwanted soap from the front of the tail, and then trim the edges of the tail and the body.

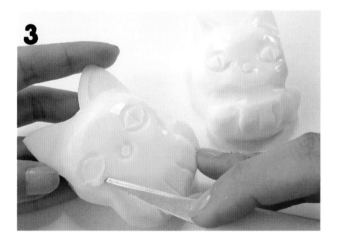

- Place the template on the soap and trace the cat's paws, eyes, and nose with a toothpick.
- *Carve the paws:* Cut the cat's paws, remove the soap from both sides of the paws, and trim the edges of them.
- *Carve the ears:* Cut a line for the inside of the ear per the template, and then slice off the inside of the ear. Do the same for the other ear.
- *Carve the nose:* Cut the nose and remove the soap around it.
- *Carve the eyes:* Cut an eye, remove the soap around the eye, and trim the edge of it. Carve a thin pointed oval shape in the eye. Do the same for the other eye.
- Slice off the soap between the face and body to create the neck. Smooth the face.

- Trim the edges of the back of the cat.
- Cut the tail as shown, remove the soap around the tail, and trim the edges of it.
- If you'd like to make a tabby cat, carve stripes in the head, the sides, the tail, the paws, and the back.
- Paint the cat with your desired colors. (See "Adding Color" on page 46.)

Squirrel

This squirrel is sure to produce smiles from everyone who spies it! The optional flower adds a sweet touch, and if you choose to make the chipmunk instead, it's also a great project to refine your coloring skills.

» SKILL LEVEL: EASY

WHAT YOU'LL NEED

» One 3- or 5-ounce (85- or 142-gram) bar soap

» Carving knife

» Small or Large Squirrel template (see page 118)

» Paring knife

» Three 4 mm plastic eyes

OPTIONAL:

» Colorants

» Small piece of soap in a different color, artificial flower stamen, short piece of wire

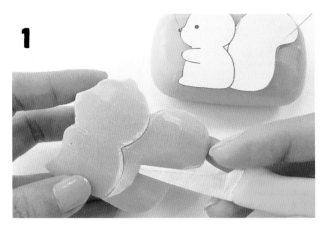

- Use the carving knife to thinly slice away the top and bottom of the soap to create a flat surface.
- Photocopy and cut out the template. Trace the squirrel shape onto your soap.
- Using a paring knife and a carving knife, cut the squirrel shape out of the soap.
- Holding your knife at a right angle, cut a curved line for the back of the squirrel. Make a slanting cut to remove the soap around the back of the squirrel. Trim the edges of the back.

- Trim the face and the head.
- Shape the front and the edges of the face to create a pointed nose.
- Remove the soap from between the ears, and then trim the edges of the ears.

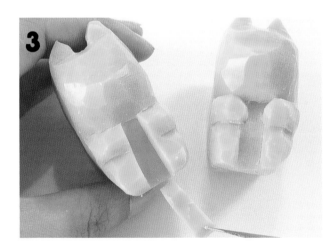

Remove the soap from between the front paws and the legs, and then trim the edges of the paws and legs.

- Trim the edge of the tail and shape it as needed.
- Make two small eyeholes and a small hole in the end of the nose. Place the plastic eyes in the holes.
- *Optional:* Make a flower: Cut a small flower shape out of the different colored soap. Shape the flower and add an artificial stamen in the same way as described for the cactus flower in Step 4 of Project 1: Miniature Cactus, on page 57.
- To make a chipmunk, cut curved lines in the ears, face, and the back of the head. Color the curved lines; I recommend using brown. (See "Adding Color" on page 46.)

Sheep

This sheep design is very simple but super-cute and suitable for white soap. This is a perfect animal carving for beginners.

» SKILL LEVEL: EASY

WHAT YOU'LL NEED

» One 3- or 5-ounce (85- or 142-gram) bar soap

» Carving knife

» Small or Large Sheep template (see page 118)

» Paring knife

OPTIONAL:

» Two 4 mm plastic eyes

» Colorants

- Use the carving knife to thinly slice away the top and the bottom of the soap to create a flat surface.
- Photocopy and cut out the template. Trace the sheep's body, horns, and ears onto your soap.
- Using a paring knife and a carving knife, cut the sheep shape out of the soap.
- Holding the carving knife at a right angle, cut the ear. Tilting the knife, remove the soap around the ear. Cut an indent in the ear. Repeat on the other ear.

- Holding the carving knife at a right angle, cut the horn and the face. Tilting the knife, remove the soap around the horn and inside the face. Repeat on the other side.
- Trim the edges of the horns and cut some lines across the horns.

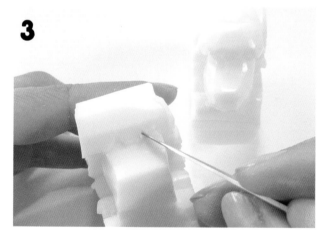

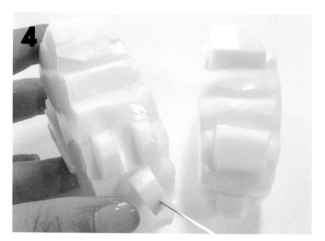

- Shape the front and the edges of the face to create a muzzle.
- Trim the edges of the head, body, and tail.

- Carve the legs. Remove the soap from between the legs and trim their edges.
- Carve half circles for the eyes or, if using the optional plastic eyes, make two small eyeholes and place the plastic eyes in the holes.
- *Optional:* Add color to the horns, ears, face, and eyes. (See "Adding Color" on page 46.)

Sea Turtle

This pretty sea turtle is very easy to make. If you want to make a land turtle, change the shape of the legs. I carved the blue transparent sea turtle out of melt-and-pour soap.

» SKILL LEVEL: EASY

WHAT YOU'LL NEED

» One 3- or 5-ounce (85- or 142-gram) bar soap

» Carving knife

» Small or Large Sea Turtle template (see page 119)

» Paring knife

» Two 4 mm plastic eyes

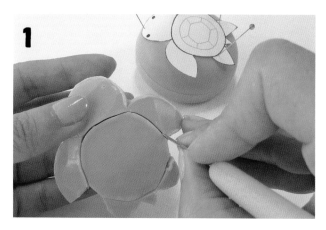

- Use the carving knife to thinly slice away the top of the soap to create a flat surface.
- Photocopy and cut out the template. Trace the sea turtle shape onto your soap.
- Using a paring knife and a carving knife, cut the sea turtle shape out of the soap.
- Holding the carving knife at a right angle, deeply cut around the shell. The depth of the line should be approximately half of the soap's total depth.

- To create the head and front legs, horizontally cut out the upper one-third of the soap.
- Then, to create the hind legs and the tail, horizontally cut out the upper half of the soap.

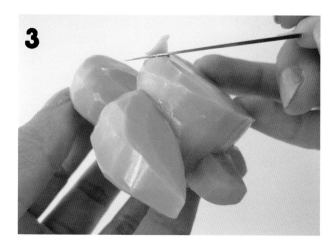

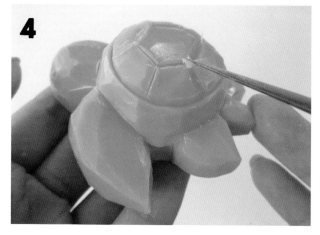

- Trim and shape the edges of the head and all legs as needed.
- Trim the tail into a pointed shape.
- Trim the shell into a dome shape.

- Following the template, carve a circle and a hexagonal pattern in the shell.
- Cut a horizontal line between the front leg and the hind leg, and remove the soap under the shell. Do the same to the other side.
- Make two small eyeholes and place the plastic eyes in the holes.

Little Insects: Ladybug, Snail & Bee

These insects are very cute and natural looking. Because insects are very small, I made these carvings small. You can make them with soap left over from other projects. I recommend making the scalloped butterfly from Carving Lesson 3 (see page 30) along with these; together, they'll make a charming display!

» **SKILL LEVEL: EASY**

WHAT YOU'LL NEED

» Small pieces of soap (to make the bee, you'll need two different colors; to make the snail, you'll need half of a bar)

» Carving knife

» Small, Medium, or Large Little Insects templates (see pages 119–120)

» Paring knife

» Black colorant (for the ladybug)

» Artificial flower stamens (for the bee)

» Black marker (if the flower stamens are not black)

LADYBUG

1

2

- Cut a piece of soap into a ⅝" (1.5 cm) slice, which will be the full height of the ladybug.
- Photocopy and cut out the template. Trace the ladybug shape onto your soap.
- Using a paring knife and a carving knife, cut the ladybug shape out of the soap.
- Trim and shape the edges as needed.

- Cut the lines for the head, body, and wings per the template.
- Cut seven circles in the wings, then remove the soap inside the circles.
- Color the head, the body, and the seven circles with black colorant.

SNAIL

1

2

- Make the snail with half of a bar of soap. Use the carving knife to thinly slice away the top of the soap to create a flat surface. Photocopy and cut out the template. Pin the template to the soap and trace the snail shape onto your soap. Using a paring knife and a carving knife, cut the snail shape out of the soap.
- Holding the carving knife at a right angle, cut a curved line around the shell. Remove the soap around the shell. Cut the whorl in the shell. Repeat on the other side.

- Trim the edges of the shell and the whorl. Next, trim the edges of the body and the head, shaping them as needed. Repeat on the other side.

BEE

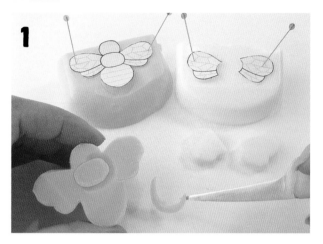

1

- Use two pieces of different-color soap. Cut the piece of soap for the body into a ⅝" (1.5 cm)-thick slice. Cut the piece of soap for the wing into a ¼" (6 mm) slice.
- Make two photocopies of the template. Using the templates, cut the bee shape and the wings out of each piece of the soap.
- Holding the carving knife at a right angle, cut the oval shape for the body, and then remove the soap around the oval. Trim the edges of the body.

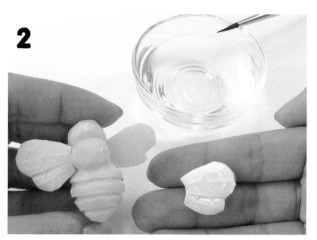

2

- Cut three horizontal lines in the bottom of the body.
- Using the knife point, cut the lines for the wing in the same pattern as the template.
- Repeat on the other wing. Add the wings to the bee with water or glue.
- Make two small holes in the head and the bottom tip of the body. Cut three artificial flower stamens (about ⅜" [1 cm] long). Put two of them in the head for the antennae. Cut off the top of the other artificial flower stamen and put it in the bottom tip of the body. (I colored the artificial stamens with a black marker.)

Miniature Cake Slice & Doughnuts

Don't discard small pieces of colorful leftover soap—use them to make these colorful soap desserts! If you make six miniature cake slices, you'll have a whole cake. And the doughnuts are so cute, you won't believe how easy they are to make!

» SKILL LEVEL: EASY

WHAT YOU'LL NEED

» Small pieces of soap (I recommend using soap in different colors.)

» Cake Slice and Doughnut templates (or round cookie cutter) (see page 120)

» Paring knife

» Carving knife

» Pin

» 2" (5 cm) of wire

» Cream soap (see page 49)

» Edible sprinkles

» Glue

CAKE SLICE

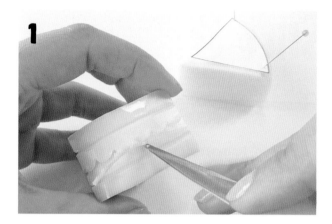

- Photocopy and cut out the templates. Trace the triangular cake slice shape onto your soap.
- Using a paring knife, roughly cut the cake slice shape out of the soap and then trim the soap into the template size.
- Carve two horizontal lines and a scallop pattern in each rectangular side of the cake slice.

- *Make a cookie:* Choose a piece of soap in a different color from what you used for the cake slice. Cut it into a slice about ¼" (6 mm) to ⅛" (3 mm) thick. Using the template, cut out the cookie shape. Then make small holes in the cookie with a pin per the template.
- Make a leaf: *Cut a piece of green or other colored* soap into a slice about ¼" (6 mm) to ⅛" (3 mm) thick. Using the template, cut out the leaf shape. Then cut a straight line in the middle of the leaf.
- *Make a cherry:* Trim a piece of red, pink, or other colored soap into a ball shape that's ¾" (1.8 cm) in diameter. Then make a small hole in the ball-shaped soap and put a piece of wire in it. Cut the wire to your desired length.
- Finally, attach the cookie, leaf, and cherry to the top of the cake slice with cream soap. (If you prefer, you can use face wash or glue instead of cream soap.)

DOUGHNUT

1

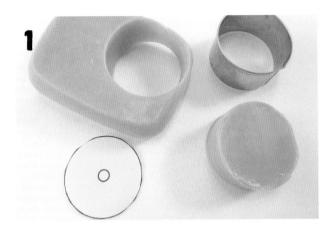

- Using a round cookie cutter or the doughnut template, cut a round shape out of the soap. If you use a cookie cutter, slice the soap thinner than the height of the cookie cutter.

2

- Using the carving knife, carve a hole in the center of the soap. Round off the edges of the doughnut. Using a knife point, carve tiny holes in the doughnut and then put the sprinkles in them. (Because edible sprinkles melt easily, don't use water or cream soap to affix them. If needed, use glue to affix the sprinkles.)

Miniature Cream Puff Swan

This cream puff is extra special because it's swan shaped. And cream soap is used for making this cream puff, so you will enjoy making it like you make a real cream puff! The cream soap is simple and easy to make.

» **SKILL LEVEL: EASY**

WHAT YOU'LL NEED

» One 3- or 5-ounce (85- or 142-gram) bar soap

» Carving knife

» Small or Large Cream Puff template (see page 120)

» Paring knife

» Spoon or sculpting tool

» Cream soap (see page 49)

OPTIONAL:

» Small piece of soap in a different color

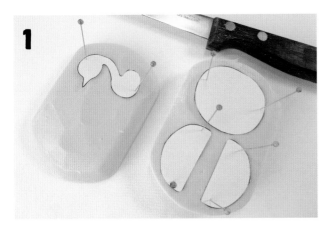

1

- Holding the bar soap with your nondominant hand, use the paring knife to cut the soap horizontally in half. Carefully cut the soap little by little so you don't accidentally cut yourself.
- Photocopy and cut out the template. Trace the parts of the cream puff onto your soap halves.

2

- Using a paring knife and a carving knife, cut the parts of the cream puff out of the soap. Trim and shape the edges as needed.
- Randomly carve indents in the wings and the circular bottom to resemble a cream puff.
- Remove the soap inside the wings with a spoon or a sculpting tool to make shallow indents. Repeat on the top of the circular bottom.

3

- Spoon some cream soap on the lower part, and add the wings and the head on top of it. (You can use face wash instead of cream soap, if you'd like.)
- *Optional:* Cut a piece of soap into a small heart shape to decorate the cream puff.
- Let the cream soap dry for 2 to 3 days.

Scalloped Frame

This fancy frame is a lovely scented décor piece that's perfect to display in your bedroom. It also makes a great gift for your family and friends. Place a favorite photo or illustration inside the frame.

» SKILL LEVEL: INTERMEDIATE

WHAT YOU'LL NEED

- » One 3- or 5-ounce (85- or 142-gram) bar soap
- » Carving knife
- » Spoon or sculpting tool
- » Toothpick
- » Small or Large Scalloped Frame template (see page 121)
- » Pin
- » Photo or illustration
- » Double-sided tape and cream soap (see page 49) or glue

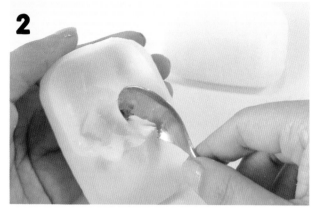

- Use the carving knife to thinly slice away the top of the soap to create a flat surface.
- Holding the bar soap with your nondominant hand, use the paring knife to cut the soap horizontally in half. Carefully cut around the side of the soap little by little so you don't accidentally cut yourself.

- Make the upper part: Using a spoon or sculpting tool, remove the soap inside the soap half until the thickness is about ¼" (6 mm).
- Make the lower part: Using the carving knife, smooth the top of the other soap half. (Don't slice off the edges.)

- Using a toothpick to make short lines or dots, divide the longer side of the upper part into four equal parts (about ½" [1.2 cm] inside the edge). Repeat on the other side.
- Next, divide the shorter side into three equal parts (about ½" [1.2 cm] inside the edge). Repeat on the other side. (Alternately, if your soap is almost the same size and shape as the template, place the template on top of your soap and trace the scalloped lines.)
- With your carving knife, cut a half circle in each part to create scalloped lines.
- Finally, cut out the inside of the upper part.

- Carve three pointed ovals and a small hole in each scallop around the frame as the template shows. Using a pin, make small holes along the scalloped edges.
- Cut your desired picture or illustration to be smaller than the soap. Place it on the top of the lower part. Attach the upper part of the frame to it.

≫ TIP

If you want to use this soap later, attach the picture with double-sided tape and attach the upper part with cream soap. If your soap will only be displayed, attach the picture and the upper part with glue.

High-Top Sneakers

These miniature sneakers are very cute. It's so fun to personalize them with your own colorants and stickers.

» **SKILL LEVEL: INTERMEDIATE**

WHAT YOU'LL NEED

» One 3- or 5-ounce (85- or 142-gram) bar soap

» Paring knife

» Carving knife

» Small or Large High-Top Sneakers templates (see page 121)

» Sculpting tool

OPTIONAL:
» Colorants and stickers

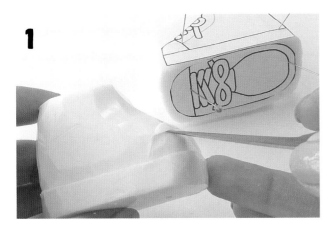

- Cut your bar of soap in half vertically with the paring knife. Use the carving knife to thinly slice away the top and the bottom of the soap to create a flat surface.
- Using the templates, cut the sneaker shapes out of your soap.
- Trim and shape the edges as needed.
- Cut a straight horizontal line all around the sneaker to create a sole. Then, tilting the carving knife to the top of the sneaker, remove the soap along the straight line.
- Cut a line across the toe to create a toe cap. Then, tilting the carving knife to the toe, remove the soap around the line.

Carve the shoelace: Using a toothpick, draw an outline of the shoelace above the toe cap per the template. Using the carving knife, cut along the outline of the shoelace and remove the soap around the shoelace, inside the bow, and below the bow. Cut lines along the outline to make it look like the shoelace is threaded through the shoe. Carve the ends of the shoelace on both sides.

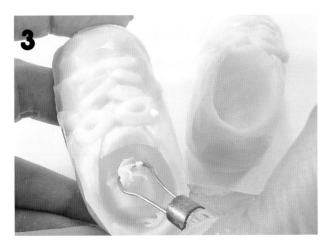

- Holding the carving knife at a right angle to the top, cut a U-shaped line inside the top. Then cut a tongue that slightly overlaps inside the U-shaped line.
- Using the carving knife and the sculpting tool, remove the soap inside the top.

- Using the knife tip, draw a curved line on both sides and draw two perpendicular lines in the back.
- Repeat these steps on the other half of the soap to make the other sneaker. (Both of the sneakers are the same; there isn't a left or right shoe in this case.)
- *Optional:* Paint the sneakers with your desired colors, and then decorate with stickers.

Party Dress

This decorative party dress is a scented hanging soap. It can be displayed on a wall or a door, and it will make a great gift for your family and friends. This dress is not only beautiful, but it is also carved using a fun technique called cut and pull out.

» SKILL LEVEL: INTERMEDIATE

WHAT YOU'LL NEED

» One 3- or 5-ounce (85- or 142-gram) bar soap

» Carving knife

» Small or Large Party Dress template (see page 121)

» Paring knife

OPTIONAL:

» 1½" (4 cm) of 18-gauge wire

» Pliers

» Rhinestones or beads

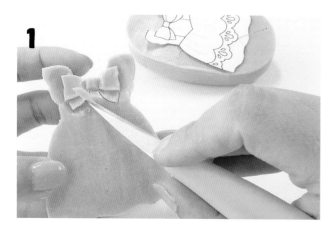

1

- Use the carving knife to thinly slice away the top of the soap to create a flat surface.
- Photocopy and cut out the template. Trace the dress shape onto your soap.
- Using a paring knife and a carving knife, cut the dress shape out of the soap.
- Place the template on the soap, then trace the bow ribbon with a toothpick. First, carve the knot of the bow (the square), and then carve the sides and tails.

2

- Trim and shape the edges as needed.
- Carve two seams below the bow, and then carve a V-shaped seam in the waist. Carve the upper scalloped line in the skirt.
- Holding your knife at a right angle to the soap, cut three teardrop shapes under the scalloped line.
- Finally, carve a scalloped line below the teardrop shapes.

3

- Holding your knife at a horizontal angle to the soap, insert the knife point under a teardrop-shaped cut and move the knife to make a horizontal cut. Then use the knifepoint to pull out the teardrop-shaped soap piece. Repeat for the other two teardrops.
- Carve two smaller teardrops on either side of the larger teardrops.

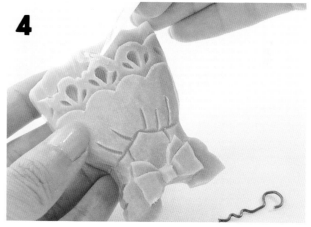

4

- Hold the dress upside down and make two incisions in each half circle of the lower scalloped line to shape the edge as shown on the template.
- Carve a few indents in the bottom edge of the dress to form a frill.
- *Optional:* Bend half of the wire with pliers into a zigzag shape and bend the rest of the wire to make a hook. Make a small hole in the top of the dress and screw the hook into the hole. (You shouldn't need to use glue to do this. Be sure the width of the zigzag is narrower than the width of the dress.)
- Decorate the dress with rhinestones or beads in any way you like. (See "Decorating with Beads" on page 48.)

Umbrella

This tiny umbrella is super-cute. I really struggled to come up with a way to put the shaft in the umbrella. Fortunately, I hit upon this idea, which is so simple and easy: make a hanging umbrella!

» SKILL LEVEL: INTERMEDIATE

WHAT YOU'LL NEED

- » One 3- or 5-ounce (85- or 142-gram) bar soap
- » Small or Large Umbrella template (see page 122)
- » Paring knife
- » Carving knife
- » Spoon or sculpting tool

- » Toothpick
- » 5" (13 cm) of 16-gauge wire
- » Pliers
- » Pin
- » Glue

OPTIONAL:
- » Rhinestones

1

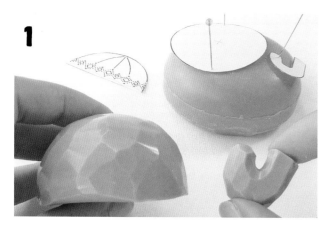

- Photocopy and cut out the template. Trace the top of the umbrella and the handle shapes onto your soap.
- Using a paring knife and a carving knife, cut the top of the umbrella and the handle out of the soap.
- Trim and shape the top of the umbrella into a dome shape. Then trim the edges of the handle.

2

- Using a spoon or sculpting tool, scoop out some of the soap from inside the dome. Make the depth of the dome half the height of the dome. (Don't remove all the soap inside the dome.) Make the sides of the dome ⅛" (3 mm) thick.

3

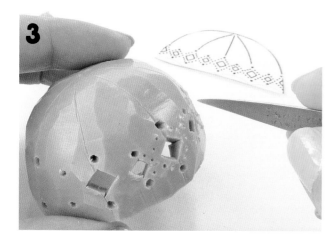

Using a toothpick, divide the top of the umbrella into eight equal parts. Draw the square patterns around the side of the umbrella as shown on the template and cut out them. Make holes with the knife point and the pin as shown on the template. Carve eight lines along the outlines. Then make a curved cut in each part of the edge to create eight pointed tips.

4

- Locate a section of the wire about 1½" (4 cm) from the end and, using your pliers, bend it a couple of times into a zigzag shape. Using the toothpick, make a small hole in the center of the top of the umbrella and insert the wire in the hole.
- Using the pliers, bend the top end of the wire into a loop. Cut off the extra length of the end. Using the toothpick, make a small hole in the top of the handle. Attach the handle to the end of the wire with glue. (Be careful not to put the wire in too deeply or the handle might break.)
- *Optional:* Decorate the top of the umbrella with rhinestones.

Teacup & Saucer

You can make your own personalized teacup-and-saucer soap carvings. I provided a pattern on the teacup template, but consider it just an example. Get creative and carve your own desired designs in the teacup, such as hearts, stripes, flowers, or whatever suits your fancy. A plain teacup is also pretty!

» SKILL LEVEL: INTERMEDIATE

WHAT YOU'LL NEED

- » Two 3- or 5-ounce (85- or 142-gram) bars of soap
- » Carving knife
- » Small or Large Teacup & Saucer template (see pages 122–123)
- » Paring knife
- » Spoon or sculpting tool

- » Toothpick
- » Pin

OPTIONAL:
- » Colorants
- » Melt-and-pour soap (about 1 ounce [28.5 grams])

- *Teacup:* Use the carving knife to thinly slice away the top of one bar of soap to create a flat surface.
- Photocopy and cut out the template. Trace the teacup top-view shape onto your soap. Using a paring knife and a carving knife, cut the teacup shape out of the soap.
- Trim the bottom as shown on the teacup side-view template.
- *Saucer:* Using the paring knife, horizontally cut the other bar of soap in half. (Cut the soap little by little so that you don't accidentally cut yourself.) Use the carving knife to thinly slice away the top of the slice of soap to create a smooth surface.
- Trace the saucer top-view template onto the slice of soap.

- *Teacup:* Trim the edges of the handle, and then cut off the soap inside the handle.
- *Saucer:* Trim the bottom as shown on the side-view template.

- *Teacup:* Using the spoon or sculpting tool and the carving knife, scoop out the soap inside the teacup, making the edge about ⅛" (3 mm) thick.
- *Saucer:* Using the spoon, make a shallow circular indent in the top of the saucer.

- *Teacup:* Using a toothpick, divide the edge of the teacup into eight equal parts. Draw three large squares and four small squares with a toothpick as shown in the template. Cut all the squares and remove the soap inside them. Using the knife point and the pin, make small holes around the corners of the squares as shown in the template. Carve a scalloped line along the edge of the teacup. Alternately, create and cut out your own design on the teacup.
- Using the carving knife, trim the edge of the teacup into a consistent thickness around the circumference of the cup. Do the same for the edge of the saucer.
- *Optional:* Add color to the teacup and saucer as desired.
- *Make tea:* Cut the melt-and-pour soap into tiny pieces. Put them in a heat-resistant container and warm in the microwave for about 20 seconds or until melted. Add soap colorant or food coloring and stir. Quickly pour it into the teacup. Leave it to set and cool for up to 60 minutes at room temperature.

Bouquet of Miniature Lilies

Many soap carvers use the flowers they create to make flower arrangements. You'll need to make stems and leaves too, but this bouquet of little lilies is super cute and perfect for gifts.

» SKILL LEVEL: INTERMEDIATE

WHAT YOU'LL NEED

- » Block of soap at least 1½" × 1½" × 1" (4 × 4 × 2.5 cm) for each lily
- » Paring knife
- » Carving knife
- » Toothpick
- » Artificial flower stamens (seven for each lily)
- » Brown marker
- » Craft glue
- » 4" (10 cm) of green ribbon for leaves (on each lily)
- » Scissors
- » Pliers and wire cutters
- » 6" (15 cm) of 18-gauge floral wire for each lily
- » Floral tape
- » 20" (50 cm) of ribbon in a color of your choice

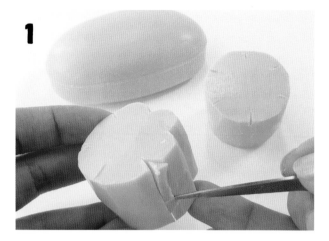

- With the paring knife, cut the soap into a block measuring 1½" (4 cm) wide × 1½" (4 cm) deep × 1" (2.5 cm) high. Trim and shape it into a cylinder with the carving knife.
- Using a toothpick, divide the top of the cylinder into six equal parts. Cut six perpendicular V-shaped grooves in the side and trim the edges of them. You now have six half circles around the circumference of the cylinder.

- Holding the carving knife at a right angle, deeply cut an inverted cone shape in the center of the top.
- Carve three petals of the first layer in the top of the soap. Starting at one V-shaped groove, cut a curved line towards the center. On the opposite side of the half circle, cut a second curved line from the V-shaped groove towards the center.
- Remove the soap around the sides of the curved lines to create the first petal. Repeat this on every other half circle to carve two more petals. (The three petals of the second layer will be placed between the petals of the first layer.)

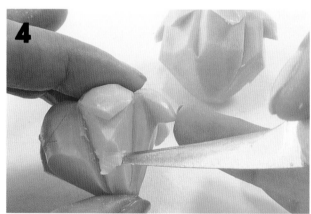

- Trim the edges of the petals.
- Cut the bottom of the soap into a pointed shape.

- Make a V-shaped cut in the underside of the petals to create the tip. Then remove the soap under the petals.
- Make six straight cuts between the sides of the petals to create a groove between each petal.
- Make a hole in the bottom of the flower to attach the stem.
- Repeat these steps to make your desired number of lilies for a bouquet.

5

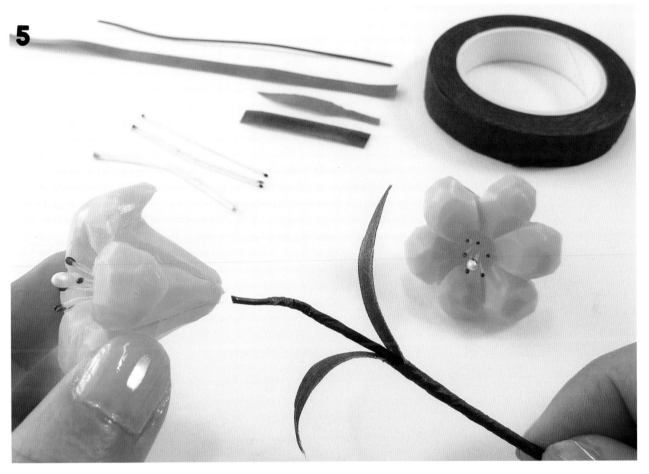

- *Add the stamens:* Make a hole in the flower with a pointed tool. Insert a stamen in the center. Then color six stamens with a brown marker. Add six brown stamens around the center stamen.

- *Make leaves:* Thinly apply craft glue to one side of the green ribbon to prevent it from fraying. Let the glue dry for about 15 minutes. Once it's dry, cut some long leaf shapes out of it with scissors. Cut the leaves so that they have long, thin petioles (thin stems that support the blade of the leaf).

- *Make stems:* Using the pliers and wire cutters, cut the floral wire into 6" (15 cm) lengths (one for each lily). Wrap the floral wire with floral tape, leaving ⅜" (about 1 cm) from the top end unwrapped. Wrap the petioles of the leaves around the exposed end of the floral wire, securing them with floral tape. Repeat with the other pieces of the wire.

- Bend the top end of the stem. Apply glue to the top end of the stem and insert the stem in the hole you created in the bottom of the flower. Make the other lilies. Cut off the stems to your desired length. Wrap all the stems together with floral tape and tie a bow with the ribbon.

Starry Cutwork Soap

Soap cutwork is a very decorative and fun technique. It's also easier than you might think. This amazing design is perfect for galaxy lovers. If you carefully attach the upper and lower parts of the soap and then fill the gaps with thin slices of soap, the finished project will look like the soap was never cut in half, and you'll leave people wondering, "How did you do that?"

» SKILL LEVEL: INTERMEDIATE

WHAT YOU'LL NEED

- » 3- or 5-ounce (85- or 142-gram) round bar soap
- » Carving knife
- » Paring knife
- » Spoon or sculpting tool
- » Small or Large Starry Cutwork template (see page 123)
- » Tape
- » Toothpick
- » Pin

OPTIONAL:
- » Cream soap or glue
- » Rhinestones

1

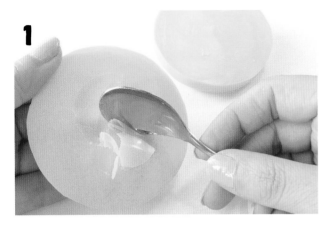

- Use the carving knife to thinly slice away the top of the soap to create a flat surface.
- Holding the soap with your nondominant hand, use the paring knife to cut the soap horizontally in half. (Carefully cut around the side of your soap little by little so you don't accidentally cut yourself.)
- Using the spoon or sculpting tool, scoop out the inside the upper part of the soap.

2

- *To make top half:* Continue removing the soap until what remains is less than ⅛" (3 mm) thick. Be careful not to break the soap. (When you hold the soap up to the light, you should be able to see your fingers clearly through the soap.)
- *To make bottom half:* Using the paring knife, smooth the cut surface. Don't trim the outer circumference.

3

Photocopy and cut out the template. Place it in the center of your hollowed-out soap and tape the template to it. Trace the moon and star shapes onto your soap with a pointed tool such as a toothpick. (You don't need to trace the other small patterns.)

4

- Cut out the moon and stars with the carving knife. (If you'd like, keep the moon- and star-shaped soap you cut.) Then cut out the other small circles and triangles as shown on the template. Make small holes with a pin.
- *Optional:* Attach the upper part to the lower part with cream soap or glue. Fill the gap between the upper part and the lower part with a leftover thin slice of the soap.
- Decorate the top of the soap with rhinestones.
- Alternately, instead of attaching the two pieces of soap, decorate the lower part with the moon and star cutouts, attaching them with cream soap or glue.

Heart Lamp

This lovely heart-shaped lamp is very simple, so it can be made quickly. If you make a plain heart lamp, it's very easy to make. And this fantastic scented lamp is perfect for bedroom décor.

» SKILL LEVEL: INTERMEDIATE

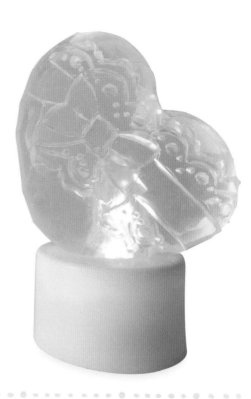

WHAT YOU'LL NEED

- » 3- or 5-ounce (85- or 142-gram) bar soap (I recommend using white soap because colored soap doesn't let enough light through. Transparent soap lets the light through well, but it's a bit difficult to carve.)
- » Carving knife
- » Small or Large Heart Lamp template (see page 123)
- » Paring knife
- » Toothpick
- » Sculpting tool, small spoon, or small metal spatula
- » LED tealight candle
- » Pin

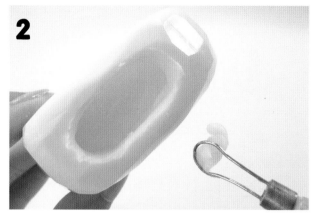

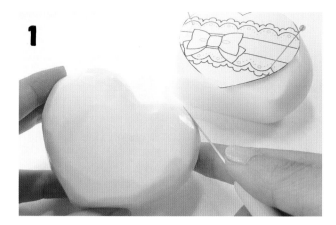

1

- Use the carving knife to thinly slice away the top and the bottom of the soap to create a flat surface.
- Photocopy and cut out the template. Trace the heart shape onto your soap.
- Using a paring knife and a carving knife, cut the heart shape out of the soap.
- Trim and shape the edges as needed.

2

- With a toothpick, draw an oval in one side of the heart. Using the sculpting tool, a small spoon, or a small metal spatula, remove the soap inside the oval. Continue removing the soap deeper inside the heart until it is about ¼" (6 mm to 8 mm) thick.
- Put the heart soap on your tealight candle to make sure the plastic flame of the candle fits inside the heart soap. (Tip: If you use transparent soap, remove the soap until the tealight candle fits inside.)

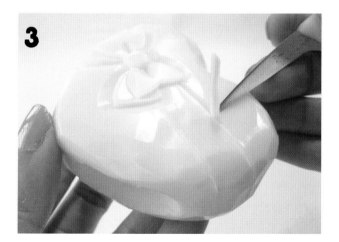

3

- Place the template on the soap, then trace the bow ribbon and horizontal straight lines with a toothpick. Carve the knot of the bow ribbon, followed by the side loops and tails. Trim the edges of the bow ribbon.
- Cut the horizontal straight lines around the bow ribbon and remove the soap around the straight lines.

4

- Smooth the soap where you will carve the scalloped lines (above the straight lines). With a toothpick, draw an outline for the scalloped line as shown on the template. Then carve the scalloped line.
- Next, carve the wavy edge along the scalloped line. Using the knife point and the pin, make small holes inside the scalloped line.
- Repeat on the lower part of the heart soap to carve the same patterns.
- Finally, place the heart soap on the LED tealight.

Orchid

Just one of these stunning flowers makes a lovely gift, or you can carve several to create a beautiful decorative wreath.

» SKILL LEVEL: INTERMEDIATE

WHAT YOU'LL NEED

» One 3- or 5-ounce (85- or 142-gram) bar soap

OPTIONAL:

» Five additional 3- or 5-ounce (85- or 142-gram) bar soaps

» Grapevine wreath, 6" (15 cm) in diameter

» Glue gun or craft adhesive

» Carving knife

» Paring knife

» Two 20" (51 cm) lengths of ribbon (in contrasting colors, textures, and/or widths)

» Seven 6 mm pearl beads

- Use a paring knife to cut the soap into a cube measuring 1½" (4 cm) wide × 1½" (4 cm) deep × ⅞" (2 cm) high.
- Holding a carving knife at a right angle, cut a small half circle in the center of one of the 1½" (4 cm) faces of the cube. This will be the pollinia of the orchid. Remove the soap around the half circle, then carve a wavy indent for the lip of the orchid.
- Holding the knife at nearly a right angle, cut a lip shape in the indent, and cut off the soap around the lip. Trim the edge of the half circle.

- In the upper right and left corners, shave down the soap slightly so the outer petals sit lower than the lip of the orchid. Carve two indents for two petals.
- Holding the knife at nearly a right angle to the soap, cut a round petal shape in each corner, then remove the soap around the petals.

- Carve three shallow indents for the three sepals: one at the top of the flower (between the two petals carved in Step 2), and one each in the lower right and lower left corners.
- Holding the knife at nearly a right angle, cut a pointed sepal in each indent, then remove the soap around the sepals.
- Draw several lines in each sepal with the knife tip.

- To finish the flower, neatly trim any unwanted soap and neaten the bottom.
- *Optional:* Repeat Steps 1 through 4 to carve five more orchids.
- Trim the bottoms so they're flat, then attach to a vine wreath with a glue gun or craft adhesive. Embellish as shown with ribbons and beads.

Carnation Arrangement

Carnations have many delicate, wavy petals. Wavy petals are very popular with carvers because they look so pretty and can be used to carve various flowers. This carnation arrangement makes the perfect gift for your friends and family.

» SKILL LEVEL: INTERMEDIATE

WHAT YOU'LL NEED

» One 3- or 5-ounce (85- or 142-gram) bar soap

» Small piece of green soap

» Paring knife

» Carving knife

» Toothpick

» 1½" (4 cm) strip of green ribbon (for each leaf)

» Craft glue

» 9" (23 cm) of 18-gauge floral wire

» Floral tape

» Small pot, bowl, or cup

1

- *Flower:* Using the paring knife and the carving knife, cut the soap into a circle (2" [5 cm] in diameter, 1" [2.5 cm] in height). Cut on a slant around the perimeter of the soap to make the lower part of the flower.
- *Calyx:* Using the paring knife, cut the green soap into a ¾" (1.8 cm) cube. Then trim one side of the cube into a rounded shape.

2

- *Flower:* Holding the carving knife at a right angle to the soap, cut a circle (1¼" [about 3 cm] in diameter) in the top of the soap. Then slightly tilt the knife and remove the soap around the circle.
- Using a toothpick, divide the circle's circumference into eight equal parts, then carve a shallow wavy indent in each part. Slightly moving the knife point up and down, cut a wavy petal in each part. Remove the soap outside the petals. The first layer of the outer petals is done.

- Carve eight shallow wavy indents around the first layer. Each indent should be carved between the petals of the first layer. Cut a wavy petal in each indent. The second layer of the outer petals is done. Note that the petals of the second layer open horizontally.

3

- *Flower:* Remove the unwanted soap on the bottom of the flower. Trim and shape the bottom of the flower as needed.
- *Calyx:* Holding the knife at a right angle, remove the soap inside the calyx. Then use a toothpick to divide the edge of the calyx into five equal parts. Cut the edge into five petal shapes. Make a hole in the bottom to attach the stem.

4

- *Flower:* Use a toothpick to divide the center of the flower into eight equal parts. Cut a wavy petal in each part, then remove the soap inside the petals. (The first row of the center is done.)
- Smooth around the center, then carve eight petals in the same way to make the second row of the center. Place each petal of the second row between the petals of the first row. Repeat to carve the third row and the fourth row. Finally, trim and neaten the center. Make a hole in the bottom to attach the stem.
- Using the green ribbon and craft glue, make some leaves in the same way as described in Project 16: Bouquet of Miniature Lilies. Be sure to cut the leaves so that they have long, thin petioles (thin stems that support the blade of the leaf).
- *Make a stem:* Wrap the floral wire with floral tape, leaving 1" (2.5 cm) from the top exposed. Wrap the petioles of the leaves around the exposed end of the floral wire, securing them with floral tape.
- Apply glue to the top end of the stem, then put the stem through the hole in the bottom of the calyx and the flower.
- Make some additional carnations in the same way. Bend the stems and put the carnations in the small pot to display.

Unicorn

This magical unicorn soap is perfect for unicorn lovers. A plain white unicorn is beautiful and traditional, or you can make your own magical unicorn by adding rainbow colors!

» SKILL LEVEL: ADVANCED

WHAT YOU'LL NEED

» One 3- or 5-ounce (85- or 142-gram) bar soap

» Small piece of soap in a different color (for unicorn's horn)

» Carving knife

» Small or Large Unicorn template (see page 124)

» Paring knife

OPTIONAL:

» Colorants

» Stickers

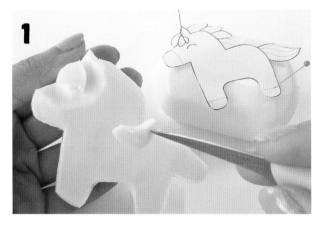

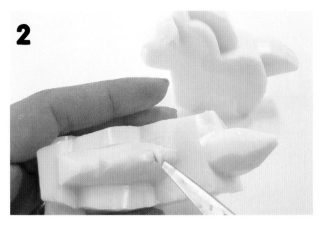

- Use the carving knife to thinly slice away the top and bottom of the soap to create a flat surface.
- Photocopy and cut out the template. Trace the unicorn shape onto your soap.
- Using a paring knife and a carving knife, cut the unicorn shape out of the soap.
- Place the template on the soap, then trace the unicorn's forelock, neck, and mane with a toothpick. Holding the carving knife at a right angle, cut the side of the forelock and remove the soap around it. Repeat on the other side.

- Holding the carving knife at a right angle, deeply cut the side of the ear and the neck along the outline, and make a straight cut in the back of the ear and the neck to remove the soap (pictured in the top unicorn). Repeat on the other side to create the unicorn's mane. Then cut on a slant on both sides of the mane to create a pointed edge along the top of the mane (pictured in the bottom unicorn). Make three incisions along the top of the mane.
- Make a shallow cut along the rear of the horse (where the rear and tail meet) and then make a horizontal cut to remove the soap on both sides of the tail. Trim and shape the tail as needed.

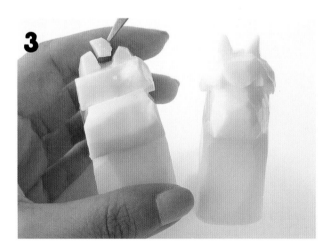

- Cut off the soap between the ears. Trim the front and the sides of the forelock.
- Trim and shape the face as needed.

4

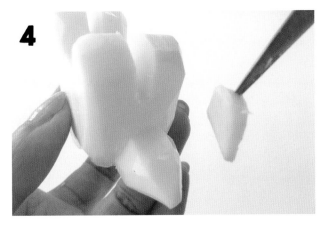

- Cut off the soap between the legs. Trim the edges of the legs. Then trim the edges of the neck and body.

5

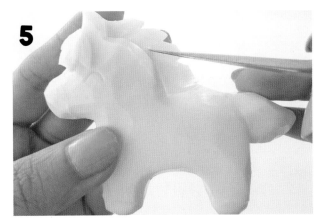

- Carve two lines in the forelock and three lines in the mane. Then, using the knife point, cut a thin line in the forelock and four thin lines in the mane. Repeat on the other side.
- Carve some curved lines in the tail. Then cut a thin line all around the muzzle and around the four feet. Carve a half circle for the eye and repeat on the other side.

6

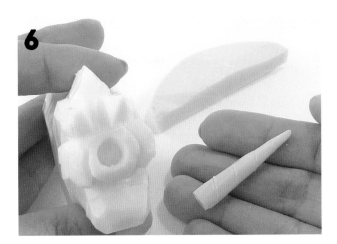

- Carve the unicorn's horn out of the small piece of soap, as shown on the template. Cut a spiral around the horn. Make a hole in the forelock, apply water to the base of the horn, and put the horn in the hole.
- *Optional:* Paint the unicorn's eyes, forelock, mane, tail, muzzle, and feet as desired, then decorate the unicorn's body with stickers.

Lock & Key

This heart-shaped lock and key design looks magical with its swirl and spiral patterns. If you find carving the swirls to be difficult, enlarge the template and make a large lock and key.

» SKILL LEVEL: ADVANCED

WHAT YOU'LL NEED

» One 3- or 5-ounce (85- or 142-gram) bar soap

» Carving knife

» Small or Large Lock and Key templates (see page 124)

» Paring knife

OPTIONAL:

» Beads and rhinestones

» Stickers

- Use the carving knife to thinly slice away the top of the soap to create a flat surface.
- Photocopy and cut out the templates. Trace the lock and key shapes onto your soap.
- Using a paring knife and a carving knife, cut the lock and key shapes out of the soap.
- *Lock:* Place the lock template on the soap, then trace the patterns inside the lock with a toothpick.
- Holding the carving knife at a right angle to the soap, cut the top edge of the heart-shaped lock. Then horizontally cut the upper part of the lock to remove the soap and create the lock shackle. Repeat on the other side.
- Holding the carving knife at a right angle to the soap, cut the keyhole along the outline.
- *Key:* Place the key template on the soap, then trace the patterns inside the key with a toothpick.
- Holding the carving knife at a right angle to the soap, cut the top edge of the heart-shaped top, then horizontally cut the upper part of the key to remove the soap and create the loop. Next cut the bottom edge of the heart-shaped top and horizontally cut the blade of the key. Repeat on the other side.
- Holding the carving knife at a right angle to the soap, cut the inside heart along the outline.

- *Lock:* Holding the carving knife at a right angle to the soap, cut a curved line in the right side of the lock (in gray on the template). Cut a perpendicular short line under the keyhole, then remove the soap along the right side of the keyhole and the curved line. (It should now look like an S-shaped groove.) Next, start to cut a curved line along the S-shaped groove (in black on the template) from under the keyhole, then cut out a small inverted cone shape at the end of the shaped groove to create a swirl.

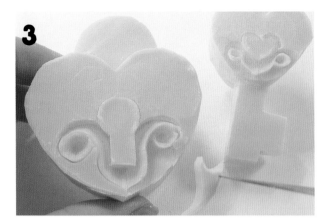

- *Lock:* Cut around the hole, then remove the soap around the hole and the curved line. Repeat on the left to carve a symmetrical swirl.
- *Key:* Carve two symmetrical swirls on both sides of the inside heart.

- *Lock:* Carve a right spiral. Start by cutting out a small inverted cone shape above the keyhole. Then holding the carving knife at a right angle, cut a curved line like half a heart around the hole. Remove the soap around the curved line. Repeat these steps to carve a left spiral.

- *Lock:* Holding the carving knife at a right angle, cut around the inverted cone shape to create a spiral.
- Then remove the soap around the hole (inside the half heart). Repeat on the left.
- *Key:* Carve two spirals above the inside heart in the same way.

- *Lock:* Carve a wing in each side of the lock as shown on the template. Smooth all the blank areas. Holding the knife at a right angle, cut a smaller keyhole inside the keyhole, then remove the soap inside the smaller keyhole.
- Cut out the inside of the shackle. Trim the edge of the shackle.
- *Key:* Carve a wing in each side of the key as shown on the template. Smooth all the blank areas. Cut out the inside of the loop at the top of the key. Trim and shape the edge of the key blade as needed.
- *Optional:* Decorate the lock and key with beads, rhinestones, and stickers as desired.

Heart Clock

Heart patterns are always popular, and a row of hearts is a traditional soap carving pattern. This fairy tale–like clock can be used as a hanging decoration. The cute clock hands are even movable!

» SKILL LEVEL: ADVANCED

WHAT YOU'LL NEED

» One 3- or 5-ounce (85- or 142-gram) round bar soap

» Small slices of soap in a different color (for clock hands)

» Carving knife

» Small or Large Heart Clock template (see page 125)

» Paring knife

» Toothpick

» 5 mm plastic eye

OPTIONAL:

» 1½" (4 cm) of 18-gauge wire

» Pliers

» 6 mm pearl beads

» 3 mm pearl beads

» Seed beads

» Glue

» Two strips of ribbon

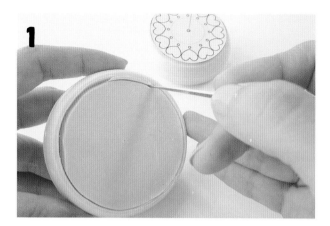

1

- Use the carving knife to thinly slice away the top of the soap to create a flat surface.
- Photocopy and cut out the template. Place the clock template in the center of the top, then trace the outer circle (the edge of the template) with a toothpick. Holding your knife at a right angle, cut a circle along the outline, then slightly remove the soap inside the circle.

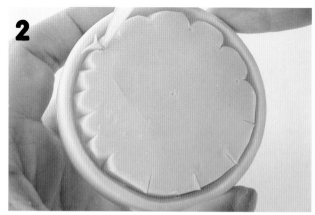

2

Use a toothpick to divide the edge of the inside circle into 12 equal parts, then use the carving knife to make 12 incisions between each part. Next, make a shorter incision in the middle of each part. Trim the edge around the incisions like the upper part of a heart.

3

Cut two curved lines between longer incisions to create the lower part of a heart. Repeat to create the remaining hearts. Then tilting the knife, cut off the soap between the hearts.

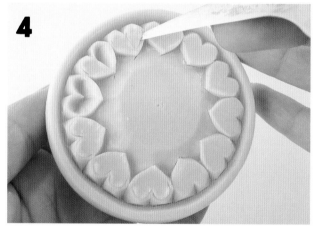

4

- Holding the carving knife at a right angle to the soap, cut two curved lines (like a half circle) inside the top edge of a heart, then cut a perpendicular straight line in the middle of the heart. Next, make a slanting cut to remove the soap inside the right side of the heart. Repeat to remove the soap inside the left side of the heart.
- Repeat with the rest of the hearts.
- Thinly slice off the soap around the bottoms of the hearts to make the center into a circle that is 1" (2.5 cm) in diameter.

5

Place the clock hands templates on the thin slices of soap (in a second color). Trace the templates onto the soap, then cut out the minute hand and the hour hand.

6

- Using the knife point, carve a hole in the center and twelve small holes around it to mark the numbers on a clock face. Put the minute hand and the hour hand in the center with a plastic eye.
- *Optional:* Make a hook by coiling half of the wire with pliers, and folding the rest of the wire into a zigzag. Make a small hole in the top of the clock, and screw the hook into the hole. (You shouldn't need glue to attach the hook.)
- Decorate the clock as desired with pearl beads and seed beads, attaching them with glue. Tie a bow on the top of the clock with a strip of ribbon. Then thread another piece of ribbon through the hook and tie a knot to hang the clock.

Gardenia with Curled Petals

Curled petals are often used for carving roses. Curled rose petals are very breakable, though, so I've designed this gardenia to carve the curled petals easily. This elegant flower soap is perfect for daily use or as a special gift!

» SKILL LEVEL: ADVANCED

WHAT YOU'LL NEED
- » One 3- or 5-ounce (85- or 142-gram) bar soap
- » Paring knife
- » Carving knife
- » Gardenia template (see page 125)

OPTIONAL:
- » Slices of green soap (for leaves)

1

- Using the paring knife and the carving knife, cut the soap into a dome shape 2" (5 cm) in diameter and 1" (2.5 cm) in height. Holding the carving knife at a right angle, cut a circle ¾" (1.8 cm) in diameter in the center. Remove the soap around the circle to make a cylinder ¼" (6 mm) high.
- Carve the first row of the center: Cut three curved lines in the top of the cylinder to create three petals as shown on the template, then slightly remove the soap inside the curved lines.

2

- Trim the edges of both sides of the petals.
- Trim outside the petal: Holding the carving knife at a nearly right angle, thinly cut the outside of the petal (on right side). Then tilting the knife, horizontally cut the base to remove the soap. Do the same to the left side of the petal.
- Trim the edges and the outside of the other two petals in the same way. (Each petal overlaps its neighboring petal.)

3

- Carve the second row of the center: Carve three petals inside the first row. Each petal should be placed between two petals of the first row.
- Carve three petals of the third row in the same way.
- Next, slice off and lower the soap around the center bud to prepare for the first outer layer.
- Carve the first outer layer: Cut three round petals around the center as shown on the template. Remove the soap around the petals. Trim the edges of the three petals.

4

- Trim under the petal: Make a thin curved cut under one side of the petal, then make a horizontal cut under the petal to remove the soap. Repeat on the other side of the petal.
- Trim under the other two petals in the same way (see the side views of the gardenia in the template).

5

- Carve the second outer layer: Carve three petals between the petals of the first outer layer in the same way (see the side views of the gardenia in the template).

6

- Carve the third outer layer: Cut around the soap under the carved petals to make six petal shapes. Place each petal between the first-layer petal and the second-layer petal.
- Trim the edges of the six petals. Make a curved cut in both sides of the petal to make a pointed tip in the petal. Repeat on the other five petals. Finally, remove the unwanted soap on the bottom.
- *Optional:* Using the slices of green soap, make some leaves, too.

Mermaid

This supercute mermaid doll requires two bars of soap. The mermaid's upper body and tail are made separately and then attached with cream soap or glue. One of the things that makes this project so fun is that the mermaid is easy to customize. You can add jewelry, change her facial expression, or customize her hairstyle or color.

» SKILL LEVEL: ADVANCED

WHAT YOU'LL NEED

» One 3- or 5-ounce (85- or 142-gram) bar soap

» One 5-ounce (142-gram) bar soap (for the mermaid's tail; use thick soap)

» Carving knife

» Mermaid templates (see page 126)

» Paring knife

» Sculpting tool (or small spoon)

» Two 4 mm plastic eyes

» Cream soap or glue

» Colorants

OPTIONAL:

» Beads or rhinestones

- *Mermaid's upper body:* Thinly slice away the top and the bottom of the soap to create a flat surface.
- Using the template, cut the upper body shape out of the soap.
- Place the template on the soap, then trace the face and the hair with a toothpick.
- Holding the carving knife at a right angle to the soap, cut the hair around the face and the shoulders along the outlines. Then, holding the carving knife at a nearly horizontal angle, slice off the soap inside the hair to create the face.
- *Mermaid's tail:* Use the carving knife to thinly slice away the top and the bottom of the second piece of soap to create a smooth surface. (Be careful not to slice away too much.)
- Using the mermaid templates, cut the tail shape out of the soap. Place the rounded rectangle template onto the top of the tail, then trace the rounded rectangle shape onto the soap. Holding the carving knife at a right angle, cut the round rectangle. Then scoop out the soap inside it with the sculpting tool or spoon.
- *Bikini top:* Using the rest of the soap, trace the bikini top shape onto the soap and cut it out. Trim and shape the edges as needed.

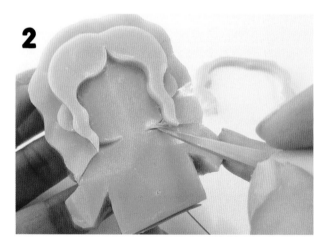

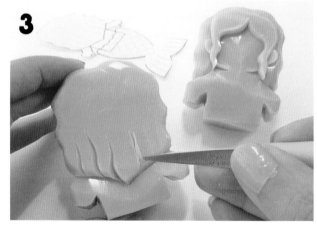

- *Upper body:* Holding the carving knife at a right angle to the soap, cut the ears. Then, holding the knife at a horizontal angle, cut off the soap around the inside of the hair and the ears. Cut a shallow indent in each ear. Trim the edges of the hair.
- Cut out the soap between the face and shoulders.

- *Upper body:* Cut a wide V-shape in the back to create the long hair, then remove the soap under the long hair. Trim the edges of the hair, and cut some long slits in the hair.

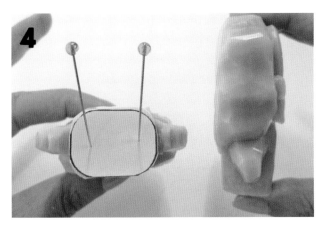

- *Upper body:* Trim and shape the arms and hands as needed. Place the round rectangle template on the bottom of the body, and trim the bottom into the template size.

- *Upper body:* Make two eyeholes in the face with a pointed tool and place the plastic eyes in them. Next, make a hole for the nose. Finally, carve the mouth.
- *Tail:* Make sure that the upper body fits in the mermaid tail. If needed, slightly trim the bottom of the body or inside the round rectangular hole of the tail to fit.
- Trim the edges of the tail and shape the tail fin. Carve scales around the tail. Use a toothpick to divide around the top of the tail into fourteen equal parts (or your desired number). Cut a half circle shape in each part, then remove the soap around them. Smooth the soap between the scales, then carve the scales of the next layer between the scales of the previous layer. Repeat until the whole tail is covered (except the tail fin).
- Make round cuts between the scales of the first layer in the top edge.
- Carve six lines in the edge of the tail fin, then repeat on the other side.

- Attach the upper body to the tail with cream soap or glue. Attach the bikini top to the body. Paint the hair with your desired color.
- *Optional:* Decorate the mermaid with beads or rhinestones.

Templates

As an alternative to photocopying the templates, go to www.quartoknows.com/page/ultimate-soap-carving to find downloadable pdfs.

Carving Lesson 1: V-Shaped Grooves and Incisions—*Leaves* (see page 24)

Two Ivy or Shamrock leaves can be made with each template.

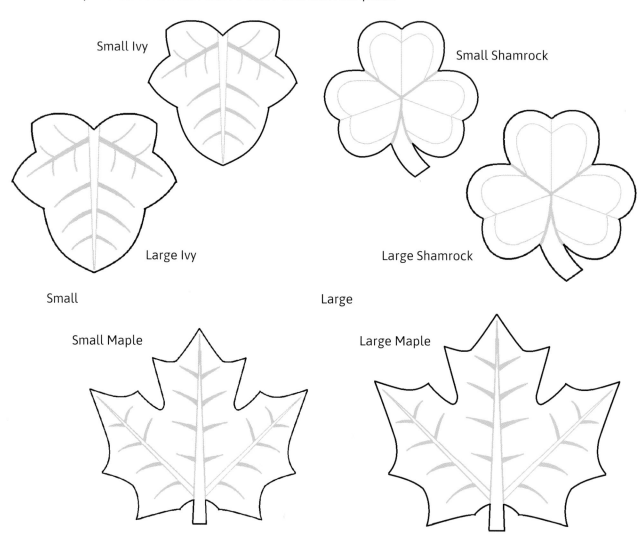

Small Ivy

Large Ivy

Small Shamrock

Large Shamrock

Small

Large

Small Maple

Large Maple

Carving Lesson 2: Triangular Patterns—*Simple Bird* (see page 28)

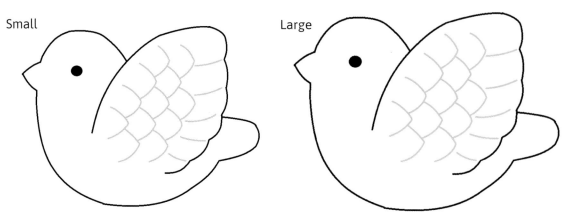

Small

Large

EXCEPT AS NOTED, USE SMALL TEMPLATES WITH 3-OUNCE (85-GRAM) BARS AND LARGE TEMPLATES WITH 5-OUNCE (142-GRAM) BARS TO MAKE ONE LESSON OR PROJECT.

Carving Lesson 3: Circular Scalloped Patterns—*Scalloped Butterfly* (see page 30)

Small

Large

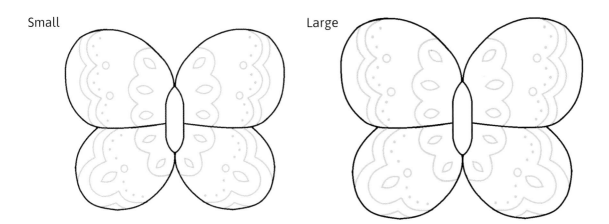

Carving Lesson 4: Delicate Waves—*Purse* (see page 32)

Small

Large

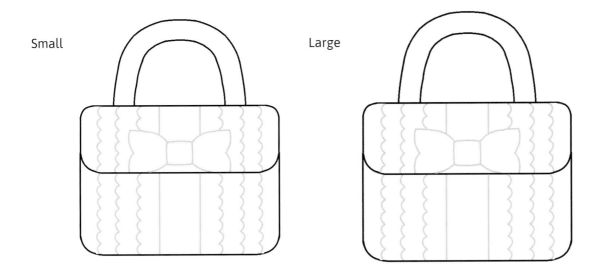

Project 3: Dachshund (see page 60)

Small

Large

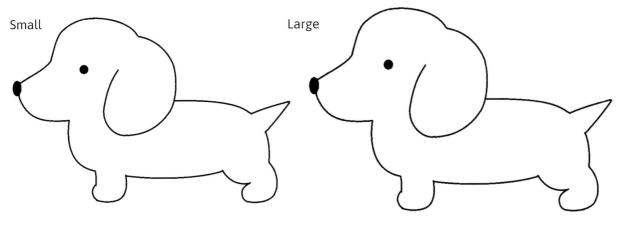

Project 4: Cat (see page 62)

Small

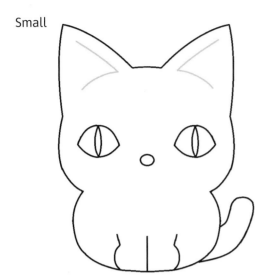

Large

Project 5: Squirrel (see page 64)

Small

Large

Project 6: Sheep (see page 66)

Small

Large

EXCEPT AS NOTED, USE SMALL TEMPLATES WITH 3-OUNCE (85-GRAM) BARS AND LARGE TEMPLATES WITH 5-OUNCE (142-GRAM) BARS TO MAKE ONE LESSON OR PROJECT.

Project 7: Sea Turtle (see page 68)

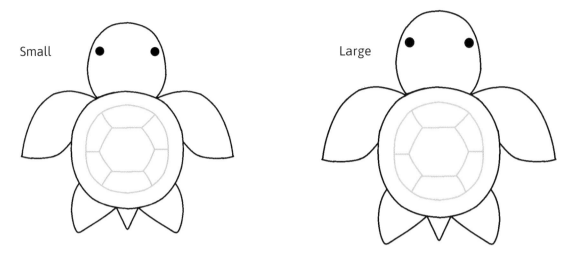

Small

Large

Project 8: Little Insects—*Ladybug* (see page 71)

All three template sizes can be used to make three Ladybugs using a 3-ounce (85-gram) bar.

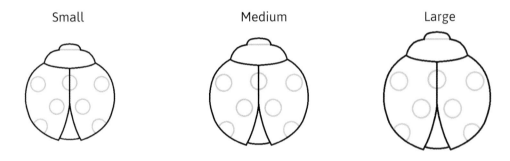

Small

Medium

Large

Project 8: Little Insects—*Snail* (see page 71)

Small and Medium templates can be used to make two Snails using a 3-ounce (85-gram) bar; the Large template can be used to make two Snails using a 5-ounce (142-gram) bar.

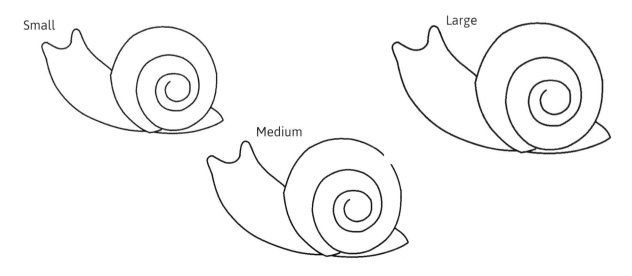

Small

Large

Medium

Project 8: Little Insects—*Bee* (see page 72)

All three template sizes can be used to make two Bees using a 3-ounce (85-gram) bar.

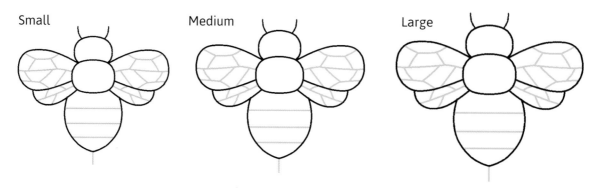

Small

Medium

Large

Project 9: Miniature Cake Slice & Doughnut (see page 73)

Use a 5-ounce (142-gram) bar to make two Cake Slices. Two Doughnuts can be made with each template size.

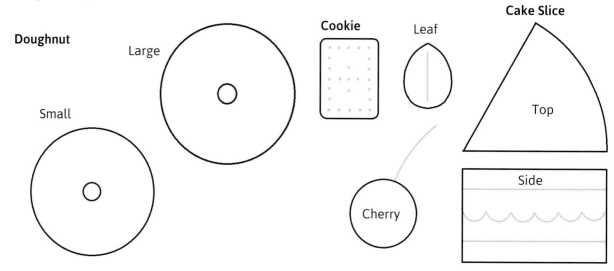

Doughnut

Large

Small

Cookie

Leaf

Cherry

Cake Slice

Top

Side

Project 10: Miniature Cream Puff Swan (see page 76)

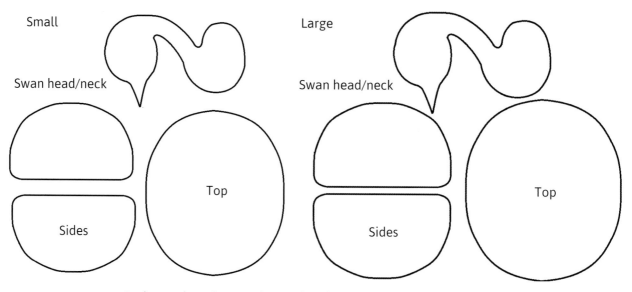

Small

Swan head/neck

Top

Sides

Large

Swan head/neck

Top

Sides

Both template sizes can be made using a 3-ounce (85-gram) bar.

EXCEPT AS NOTED, USE SMALL TEMPLATES WITH 3-OUNCE (85-GRAM) BARS AND LARGE TEMPLATES WITH 5-OUNCE (142-GRAM) BARS TO MAKE ONE LESSON OR PROJECT.

Project 11: Scalloped Frame (see page 78)

This project can be made without a template. Refer to the template as a guide to carving the scallop shapes.

Small   Large

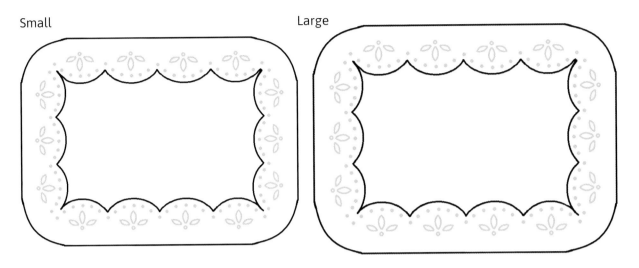

Project 12: High-Top Sneakers (see page 80)

Two High-Top Sneakers (left and right) can be made with each template.

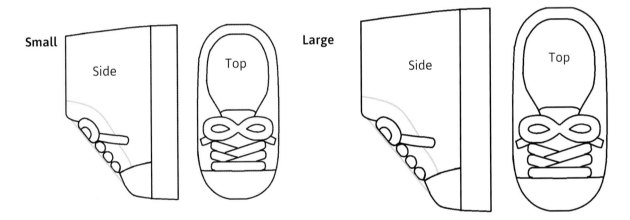

Project 13: Party Dress (see page 82)

Small   Large

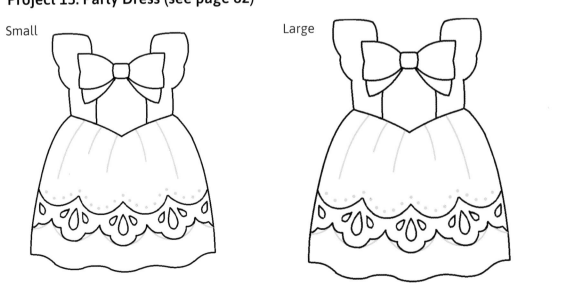

Project 14: Umbrella (see page 84)

This project can be made with either round or rectangular soap.

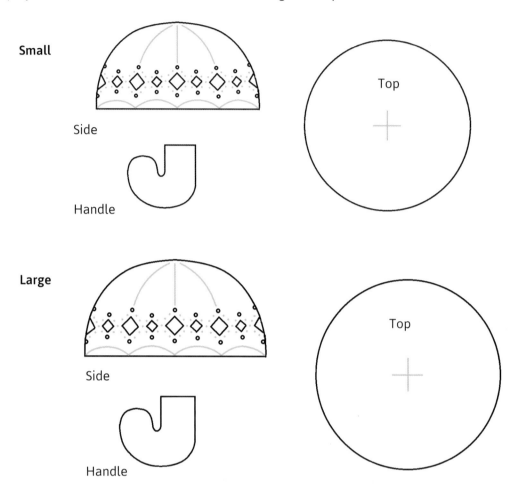

Small

Side

Handle

Top

Large

Side

Handle

Top

Project 15: Teacup & Saucer (see page 86)

Both Small and Large Saucers and the Small Teacup can be made using a 3-ounce (85-gram) bar; the Large Teacup can only be made using a 5-ounce (142-gram) bar.

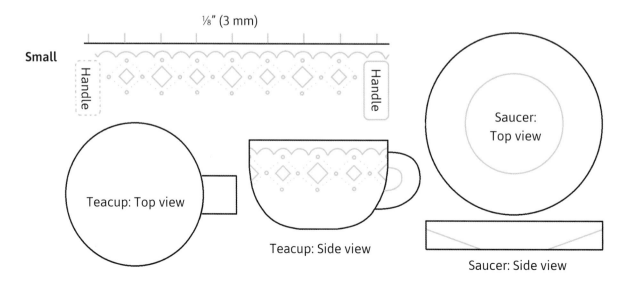

⅛" (3 mm)

Small

Handle

Handle

Teacup: Top view

Teacup: Side view

Saucer: Top view

Saucer: Side view

EXCEPT AS NOTED, USE SMALL TEMPLATES WITH 3-OUNCE (85-GRAM) BARS AND LARGE TEMPLATES WITH 5-OUNCE (142-GRAM) BARS TO MAKE ONE LESSON OR PROJECT.

Project 15: Teacup & Saucer (see page 86)

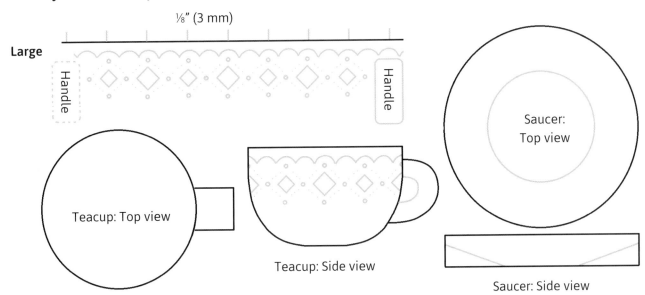

⅛" (3 mm)

Large

Handle

Handle

Teacup: Top view

Teacup: Side view

Saucer: Top view

Saucer: Side view

Project 17: Starry Cutwork Soap (see page 92)

Both template sizes should be used with round soap.

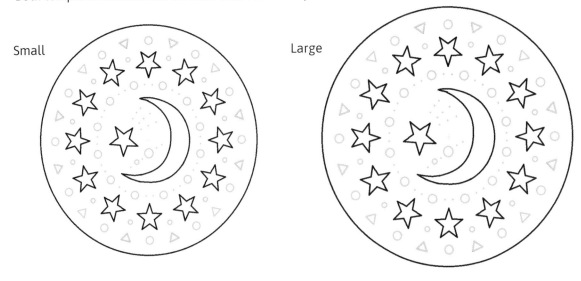

Small

Large

Project 18: Heart Lamp (see page 94)

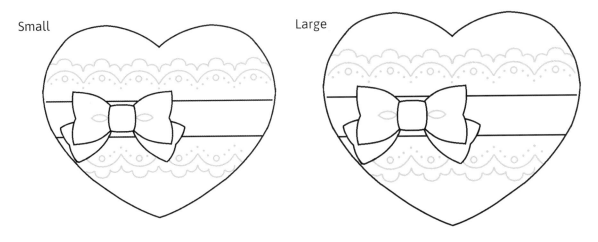

Small

Large

Project 21: Unicorn (see page 101)

Small

Large

Project 22: Lock & Key (see page 104)

Each size of Lock and Key can be made from one bar of soap.

Key

Small

Large

Lock

Small

Large

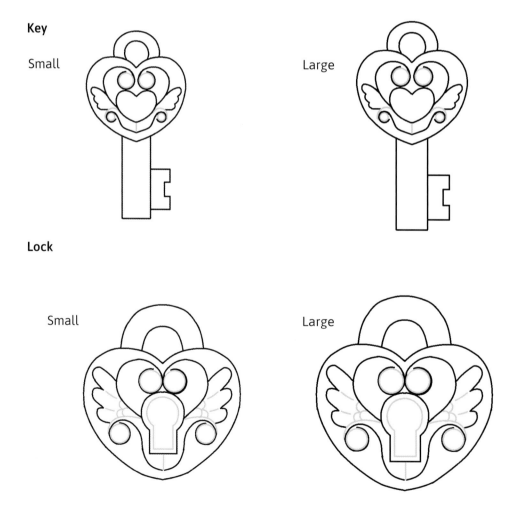

**EXCEPT AS NOTED, USE SMALL TEMPLATES WITH 3-OUNCE (85-GRAM) BARS AND
LARGE TEMPLATES WITH 5-OUNCE (142-GRAM) BARS TO MAKE ONE LESSON OR PROJECT.**

Project 23: Heart Clock (see page 107)

Both template sizes should be used with round soap.

Small   Large

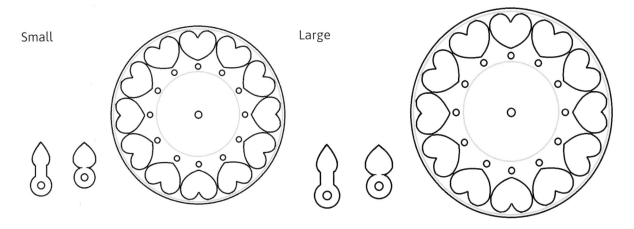

Project 24: Gardenia with Curled Petals (see page 110)

This project can be made without a template. Refer to the template as a guide to carving the petals.

Side   Side

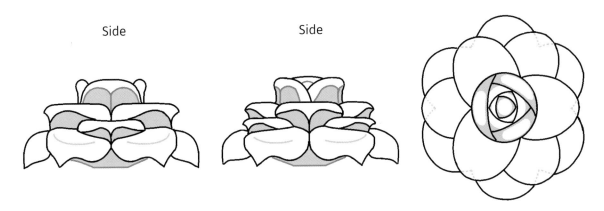

Project 25: Mermaid (see page 114)

The mermaid's body can be made with a 3-ounce (85-gram) bar.
Use a 5-ounce (142-g) bar to carve the mermaid's tail.

Front   Back

**EXCEPT AS NOTED, USE SMALL TEMPLATES WITH 3-OUNCE (85-GRAM) BARS AND
LARGE TEMPLATES WITH 5-OUNCE (142-GRAM) BARS TO MAKE ONE LESSON OR PROJECT.**

Acknowledgments

Special thanks to acquisitions editor Joy Aquilino, art director Marissa Giambrone, project manager Renae Haines, managing editor John Gettings, development editor Amy Kovalski, copyeditor Constance Santisteban, marketing manager Lydia Anderson, and the entire Quarto Group.

About the Author

Makiko Sone, better known to her followers as Mizutama Soap, demonstrates cute, fantastic, and easy-to-make soap carving projects on her YouTube channel, mizutama.soap, and sells supplies on her Etsy shop, MizutamaStudio. Her most popular video has gotten more than 1 million views. She lives in Japan.

INDEX